WEIGHING IN
Nutrition and Weight Management

WEIGHING IN

Nutrition and Weight Management

LESLI J. FAVOR

mc Marshall Cavendish

Benchmark Books
Marshall Cavendish
99 White Plains Road
Tarrytown, NY 10591-9001
www.marshallcavendish.us

All Internet sites were available and accurate when sent to press.

Library of Congress Cataloging-in-Publication Data

Favor, Lesli J.
  Weighing in : nutrition and weight management / by Lesli J. Favor.
     p. cm.
  Summary: "Provides a basic, comprehensive introduction to weight
management, including information on using the body-mass index formula and
the food pyramid to make healthy food choices"—Provided by publisher.
  Includes bibliographical references and index.
  ISBN-13: 978-0-7614-2555-7
  1. Weight loss. 2. Nutrition. 3. Body weight—Regulation. I. Title.

RM222.2.F378 2007
613.2--dc22
2006101930

Digestive system and weight loss illustrations by Ian Warpole
Photo credits: Cover photo by Stone/Getty Images

The photographs in this book are used by permission and through the courtesy of: *Getty Images*: Stone, 3; Corbis: Bo Zaunders, 6; Rick Gomez, 18; Pat Doyle, 22; Michael A. Keller, 26; Roger Ressmeyer, 76; *The Image Works*: Bob Daemmrich, 12; Jeff Greenberg, 60; *Alamy*: Bubbles Photo Library, 16; Chris Rout, 48; *Photo Edit*: David Young Wolff, 20; Michael Newman, 38; Mark Richards, 53; *SuperStock*: age footstock, 65.

Editor: Deborah Grahame
Publisher: Michelle Bisson
Art Director: Anahid Hamparian
Series Design: Becky Terhune

Charts in the appendixes are reprinted with permission from Dietary Reference Intakes for Energy, Carbohydrate, Fiber, Fat, Fatty Acids, Cholesterol, Protein, and Amino Acids (Macronutrients) © 2005 by the National Academy of Sciences, courtesy of the National Academies Press, Washington, D.C.

Printed in Malaysia

3 5 6 4 2

CONTENTS

Myth: *An overweight person will always be overweight.*

Fact: *An overweight person can achieve a healthy weight through lifestyle changes.*

1

THE NEED FOR WEIGHT MANAGEMENT

You may have noticed that the subject of body weight gets a great deal of attention in the media, in health education, and in our private lives. Most people know what they weigh, whether in general terms or down to the last half pound. In a nationwide study of U.S. high school students, 62 percent of girls and 28 percent of boys said they were trying to lose weight. [1] Clinically, not all of these teenagers are overweight, though experts estimate that 10 to 15 percent of American adolescents are overweight or at risk of overweight. [2] However, overweight among young people is steadily increasing. The number of overweight adolescents tripled [3] between the late 1970s and 2000, according to Richard Lowry of the Centers for Disease Control. [4]

Percentage of Overweight Adolescents, Ages 12–19

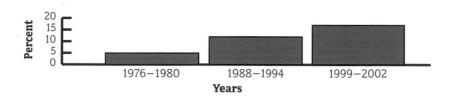

Adolescents are not the only group struggling with excess weight. Between the late 1970s and 2002, the number of obese adults doubled, from 15 to 31 percent of people age twenty and over. Young children, too, are showing an increase in overweight, from 7 percent of six- to eleven-year-olds in 1980 to 16 percent in 2002. [5] The increase in obesity among people of all ages has caused medical experts to refer to an obesity epidemic. They use this term because this medical condition is widespread, increasing rapidly, and carries many health risks. For these reasons, experts agree that weight management is crucial to the health of affected individuals.

WHAT IS OBESITY?

The conditions of overweight and obesity are not just about higher numbers on the scales. More important, they concern the health risks associated with excess body fat. Basically, an overweight person has more body fat than is healthy for his or her height. An obese person has a great deal more body fat than is healthy. For medical purposes, the condition of being overweight or obese is determined based on a person's body mass index (BMI). In adults a BMI between 18.5 and 24.9 is considered healthy. A BMI between 25 and 29.9 indicates a condition of overweight. A BMI of 30 or greater indicates obesity.

You can calculate your own BMI using your weight and your height. Your BMI can give you a good idea of what your body fat is in relation to your height, and it will tell you if you are overweight or obese. To determine your BMI, divide your weight in pounds by your height in inches squared. Multiply that by 703. The formula looks like this:

$$BMI = \left(\frac{\text{weight in pounds}}{(\text{height in inches}) \times (\text{height in inches})} \right) \times 703$$

For example, suppose a woman weighs 140 pounds and is 5'4" tall. Her BMI would be 24. A man who weighs 155 pounds and stands 5' 10" tall has a BMI of 22.2.

After calculating their BMI, they can consult a reference table to see if their BMI falls within a healthy range for their height and weight. Consider the following table.

BODY MASS INDEX (BMI) REFERENCE TABLE

A healthy BMI falls in the range of 18.5–24.9. A BMI of less than 18.5 is considered underweight; a BMI between 25 and 29.9 is considered overweight; a BMI of 30 or greater is considered obese.

BMI	Healthy			Overweight			Obese			
	19	22	24	25	27	29	30	33	36	39
Height					Body Weight (pounds)					
4'10"	91	105	115	119	129	138	143	158	172	186
4'11"	94	109	119	124	133	143	148	163	178	193
5'0"	97	112	123	128	138	148	153	168	184	199
5'1"	100	116	127	132	143	153	158	174	190	206
5'2"	104	120	131	136	147	158	164	180	196	213
5'3"	107	124	135	141	152	163	169	186	203	220
5'4"	110	128	140	145	157	169	174	192	209	227
5'5"	114	132	144	150	162	174	180	198	216	234
5'6"	118	136	148	155	167	179	186	204	223	241
5'7"	121	140	153	159	172	185	191	211	230	249
5'8"	125	144	158	164	177	190	197	216	236	256
5'9"	128	149	162	169	182	196	203	223	243	263
5'10"	132	153	167	174	188	202	209	229	250	271
5'11"	136	157	172	179	193	208	215	236	257	279
6'0"	140	162	177	184	199	213	221	242	265	287
6'1"	144	166	182	189	204	219	227	250	272	295
6'2"	148	171	186	194	210	225	233	256	280	303

Source: Adapted from National Heart, Lung, and Blood Institute, "Body Mass Index Table."
*For the metric calculation of the BMI formula and Metric Conversion Chart, see page 98.

A healthy BMI falls in the range of 18.5 to 24.9. A BMI less than 18.5 is considered underweight, and a BMI between 25 and 29.9 is considered overweight. Someone with a BMI of 30 or greater is considered obese.

In most cases the BMI number gives a good indication of a person's amount of stored body fat. The BMI formula, however, does not distinguish between body weight gained from muscle and weight gained from fat. As a result, some heavily muscled athletes may have a BMI score in the unhealthy range when in fact they are not overweight. If you think your BMI is cause for concern, the best thing to do is talk to your family doctor or a school nurse. In this book you will find out more about determining your own healthy body weight in chapter 2.

BMI-FOR-AGE

When physicians assess the body mass index (BMI) of children and teenagers, they use different terms than those for adults. For young people, a BMI above a normal weight-for-height is *at risk of overweight* or *overweight*. The term *obese* is not used for this age group. A BMI below a normal weight is *underweight*.

BMI for children and teens is often called BMI-for-age. The BMI-for-age takes into account a person's age and gender. As young people grow up, their body fat changes, depending on the stage of their development. BMI decreases during the preschool years and then increases as children grow older. Gender is also a factor. Girls and boys have different levels of body fat at different stages of growth. As a result, the standard BMI reference table for adults is not the best tool for evaluating young people.

BMI-for-age is calculated using gender-specific growth charts. (These can be found in Appendixes A and B in the back of this book.) The charts are designed for young people two to twenty years old. If you mapped your age and BMI on the appropriate chart (girls or boys), you would identify which percentile you are in. In the charts, a percentile is a number used to show what percentage of girls or boys your age have a lower BMI than yours. For instance, suppose your BMI is in the 70th percentile. This means that 70 percent of people your age and gender have a lower BMI. If your BMI is in the 50th percentile, then half the people your age and gender have a lower BMI.

Using the appropriate growth chart, physicians can determine whether a young person is underweight, normal weight, at risk of overweight, or overweight. The charts use percentiles as cutoff points between the categories. Notice that the lowest curved line on the charts marks the 5th percentile. If your age and BMI intersect at or below this percentile, you are considered underweight. The highest curved line marks the 95th percentile. If your age and BMI intersect at or above this percentile, you are considered overweight. The weight assessment chart lists the percentiles that health professionals use to assess young people's weights.

Weight assessment using BMI-for-age

Underweight	BMI-for-age less than 5th percentile
Normal	BMI-for-age 5th percentile to less than 85th percentile
At risk of overweight	BMI-for-age 85th percentile to less than 95th percentile
Overweight	BMI-for-age greater than or equal to 95th percentile

A mother reads with her son. Children learn habits from their parents, including attitudes toward food and patterns of eating.

WHO IS AT RISK FOR BECOMING OBESE?

Obesity occurs among people of all ages, races, ethnicities, and of both genders. Studies show that obesity rates vary among different subgroups of the U.S. population.[6] More adult women than men are obese, for example. Among women, more blacks are obese than Hispanic or white women. Among men, however, rates of obesity vary little based on race or ethnicity. The data show different findings for children and adolescents. Among people ages twelve to nineteen, Mexican-Americans and blacks are slightly more likely to be obese than non-Hispanic whites.

Still, race/ethnicity is not the only factor used by experts to track obesity trends. Rates of obesity vary by region of the country. In 2005, three states reported that 30 percent or more of their residents were obese. Fourteen states reported that 25 percent to 29 percent of their residents were obese. Over half of the states—29 of them—reported a 20 percent to 24 percent obesity rate. Only four states reported an obesity rate of 15 percent to 19 percent.[7]

What do all these data mean to you? For one thing, it is important to remember that each person is an individual, not a statistic. Being female or living in Texas, for instance, doesn't mean you are fated to be overweight. Excess weight is not caused by a certain sex, ethnicity, or place of residence. Most often, excess weight results from eating more calories than you need, causing your body to store the extra energy as fat. Certain environmental factors may influence your eating and exercising habits, but the choices of how to eat and how active to be are nevertheless your own.

WHAT CAUSES WEIGHT GAIN?

At the simplest level, weight gain happens when there is a greater intake of energy (calories) than the body expends, or uses. The body stores the extra energy as fat, resulting in excess body weight. The condition of being overweight or obese develops over a long period of time, not overnight. That said, the issue of obesity is more complex than just counting calories. A variety of factors influences the choices that an individual makes leading to a particular body weight.

FACTORS THAT INFLUENCE BODY WEIGHT

- energy intake versus output
- genes
- metabolism
- socioeconomic status
- environment and behavior [8]

Energy intake versus output

The issue of body weight boils down to balance. To maintain a healthy weight, you need to consume enough calories to fuel your body without having unused calories left over to be stored as fat.

Weight gain results from consuming more calories per day

than you use per day, on average—weight loss from consuming fewer calories than you use. A steady weight indicates a balance of calories consumed and calories used.

Genes

In certain cases, genes can determine obesity. Such hereditary causes of excess weight usually involve endocrine problems, chromosomal abnormalities, or metabolic disorders. Examples include Cushing's syndrome, growth hormone deficiency, spina bifida, and muscular dystrophy. Prader-Willi syndrome is a genetic disorder that includes, among other attributes, an urge to eat constantly, which leads to obesity. Bardet-Biedl syndrome, too, counts obesity among its attributes. Fewer than 2 percent of obese people have a metabolic disorder or hormonal imbalance. [9]

Metabolism

Metabolism is the total of all the chemical processes that keep your body cells healthy and keep you alive. Some of these chemical processes break down molecules to release stored energy. Others combine molecules to make substances your body needs to function.

An adult's resting metabolic rate, or RMR, is the amount of energy expended when awake but resting, not digesting food, and neither hot nor cold. On average, a young man has an RMR that burns about 60 calories per hour, while a young woman has an RMR that burns about 53 calories per hour. Physical exercise, digestion of food, and raised body temperature are factors that increase the metabolic rate above the RMR. When people are sleeping, their metabolic rate is about 10 percent less than their RMR.

Is there such a thing as a "fast metabolism" that burns more calories than normal or a "slow metabolism" that burns fewer calories? Studies of resting metabolic rates suggest that the answer is no. RMRs vary only in regard to the surface area of the individual—that is, how large the body is—and how old the person is. For instance, a large adult has a slightly higher RMR than a small adult. Children who are still growing have RMRs about twice as high in relation to their size as the RMRs of elderly people. Studies fail to show that some people are "naturally thin" or "naturally fat" due to their metabolic rates.

Socioeconomic status

According to the U.S. Department of Health and Human Services, overweight and obesity are more common in people with lower family incomes than those with higher incomes. Women of a lower socioeconomic status (income less than or equal to 130 percent of the poverty threshold) are about fifty times more likely to be obese than those in a higher socioeconomic status. Non-Hispanic white adolescents from lower income families are more likely to be overweight than those from higher income families. Among black and Hispanic adolescents, however, family income does not correlate to a likelihood of overweight or obesity. [10]

Environment and behavior

The environment in which people live promotes behaviors that affect body weight. People living in the United States, for example, are surrounded by sources for fast, inexpensive, energy-rich foods. Geographic region matters little. The smallest towns and the largest cities alike are dotted with fast food restaurants offering so-called value meals—low-priced but not low-calorie. A family may be able to buy fast food and sodas for dinner for less than they can obtain lean meat, vegetables, fruits, and milk at the supermarket.

Nutrition is often not the deciding factor in teens' food choices.

Besides fast food, sugary and fatty snacks are more readily available than in the past. Vending machines, convenience stores, shopping malls, supermarkets, coffee shops, and other places ensure that wherever people go, they can grab a snack, even in school hallways. Nutrition is not necessarily a factor in merchants' decisions of what to sell or in consumers' decisions of what to buy.

Not only that, but the trend toward larger portion sizes promotes indulgent eating habits. Everything from french fries to pizzas to cookies to soft drinks have been supersized, partly to cater to customers' desire for more value for the dollar. Restaurants serve single meals on big platters, advertise all-you-can-eat buffets, and give unlimited refills on soft drinks. Consumers have grown accustomed to large or unlimited portions and forget that such great amounts of food will easily exceed their calorie needs for the day.

Americans are living in a "toxic food environment" that places them at great risk for obesity, argues Kelly D. Brownell, director of the Yale Center for Eating and Weight Disorders, citing the following:

The yearly marketing budget of McDonald's is $1.1 billion, and of Coca-Cola, $866 million, and these are just two companies. The budget of the National Cancer Institute to promote healthy eating is just $1 million. . . . It is not a fair contest, and the outcome, a world with diets growing rapidly worse, cannot be considered surprising. [11]

Along with all this fast, inexpensive, calorie-rich food, the typical American lifestyle includes very little physical activity. Regrettable budget cutbacks in school recess programs and required physical education classes have curtailed many young people's ability to be physically active during the school day. And according to the Centers for Disease Control, more than 26 percent of adults have no leisure-time activity at all. [12] Leisure activities, or exercise just for the fun of it, include walking, running, biking, swimming, team sports, tennis, dancing, and similar pursuits.

Technology, too, contributes to sedentary lifestyles. Shopping on the Internet, taking elevators instead of stairs, playing video or computer games instead of playing sports, and driving a car instead of riding a bike or walking are just a few examples.

THE GOOD NEWS

Obesity exists in epidemic proportions. The good news, however, is that each individual has direct control over his or her body weight. Determining a healthy body weight, learning about nutrition and healthful eating habits, and becoming physically active are key elements of lifelong weight management. These topics are looked at more fully in the chapters that follow.

> **Myth:** *The more you weigh, the fatter you are.*
> **Fact:** *Body weight reflects not just body fat, but muscles and height, among other factors.*

2
WHAT IS A HEALTHY WEIGHT FOR *YOU?*

Studies show that 40 percent of all adolescents are trying to lose weight.[1] Are all of these young people overweight? Not at all. In fact, only about 10 to 15 percent of children and adolescents are overweight.[2]

When it comes to assessing your own weight, how can you find out if you are at a healthy weight? It helps to consult body mass index charts or height/weight charts. These tables use standards established by doctors and other professionals to provide guidelines for the general population. However, no two bodies are alike in their distribution of bone, muscle, and fat. Lifestyle and genetics also play a part in what you weigh. Learning about all these factors will help you determine a healthy body weight for you.

BODY FAT

Each body, male or female, needs some fat stores to remain healthy and to function properly. Fat provides energy and is necessary for cell membrane structure, blood-clotting functions, and the transportation of fat-soluble vitamins. Individuals who try to rid their bodies of all fat can permanently damage their bodies. For instance, when a female who has gone through puberty falls below about 22 percent body fat, her body may stop menstruating (getting a period every month). If she starts eating healthfully and regains the necessary body fat, her period will usually resume.

So how much body fat do you have right now? How much do you need, and how much is too much?

To determine precisely how much fat your body is storing right now, you might get a professional body fat analysis. This

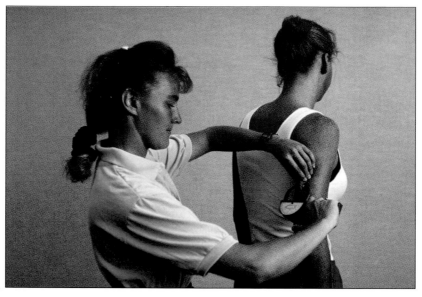

Using a digital skin fold caliper, a health-care professional measures this young woman's body fat percentage.

type of test requires special equipment to weigh a person underwater. Another test uses a method called X-ray absorptiometry to measure body fat. These tests are the most accurate, but they are expensive and can be inconvenient for the average person.

An alternative to calculating precisely how much body fat you have is to determine a healthy weight for you that takes into account your body fat. The National Institutes of Health recommends a method of determining a healthy weight that you can do on your own, without special equipment. This method takes into account your body mass index, your waist measurement, and your individual medical history.

BODY MASS INDEX

As you learned in chapter 1, an adult's body mass index (BMI) is calculated using weight and height. A young person's BMI-for-age is calculated using age and gender. The first step in determining a healthy weight for you is determining your BMI or BMI-for-age, as appropriate.

Adults can use the BMI Reference Table in chapter 1 to determine how healthy their BMIs are. A healthy BMI falls in the range of 18.5 to 24.9. An adult with a BMI less than 18.5 is considered underweight, while someone with a BMI between 25 and 29.9 is considered overweight. An adult with a BMI of 30 or greater is considered obese.

Children and teenagers can use the growth charts for BMI-for-age (pages 92-93) to determine whether they are under-weight, normal weight, at risk of overweight, or overweight.

In addition to determining your BMI or BMI-for-age, you should take into account your waist measurement and per-sonal medical history when evaluating your body weight.

WAIST MEASUREMENT

Some of the health problems associated with being overweight or obese are high blood pressure, diabetes, abnormal levels of blood fats, and coronary artery disease. Measuring the circumference of your waist can help you evaluate your health. Determine whether your body tends to store excess fat around your waist and upper body or whether you store excess fat around your thighs and lower body. Excess fat in the waist/abdominal area carries

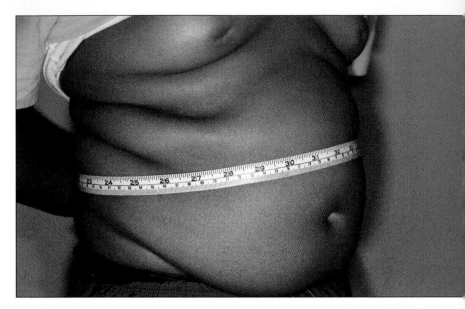

Excess fat stored in the abdominal area indicates an increased risk for health problems.

greater risks of health problems than fat stored lower in the body.

The most useful waist measurement is to measure your abdomen just above the hip bones. A measurement greater than 40 inches (101 cm) for men or 35 inches (89 cm) for women indicates excess fat stored in the abdominal area. Because this body type is round in the middle, it is often referred to as apple-shaped. Apple-shaped bodies have a higher risk of fat-related health problems than pear-shaped bodies, the ones that store fat lower down in the thighs and buttocks.

MEDICAL HISTORY

A third approach to evaluating your health in relation to body weight is to consider your personal medical history. A family history of obesity, cardiovascular disease, diabetes, or high blood pressure indicates that you are at higher risk for developing such a health problem. Being overweight increases this risk.

There are medical causes of being overweight, though they do not occur frequently. One medical cause of weight gain is Cushing's syndrome, a disorder caused by prolonged exposure to high levels of the hormone cortisol. It is most common in adults age twenty to fifty and occurs in only about ten or fifteen of every million people. Obesity is associated with certain genetic disorders such as Prader-Willi syndrome and Bardet-Biedl syndrome, as discussed in chapter 1. A medical doctor is necessary to diagnose these disorders.

Many young people wonder if they are destined to be overweight or obese because of a family history of overweight or obesity. The answer to this question is not simple. Researchers report a tendency for obesity to run in families, but they caution that the connection between genetics and obesity is unclear. A person may become overweight or obese because of family eating and lifestyle habits acquired early in life, not because of genetics.

A family that routinely eats large portions of foods, especially fatty fast foods and junk foods—foods low in nutritional content—is more likely to be overweight than a family that eats reasonable portions of grains, lean meats, vegetables, and fruits. To an outside observer it may look as if one family is genetically programmed to be fat while another is not, but a realistic look at their patterns of eating suggests otherwise.

In addition to genetic factors, your personal medical history includes lifestyle factors. If you are routinely physically active, you will use more energy from the food you eat. As a result, your body will store less energy as fat. In contrast, sitting at a desk in school or in an office is considered sedentary, or inactive. Sedentary persons are more likely to accumulate excess body fat.

Certain medications have been shown to promote weight gain in some people. A few examples include certain steroids, antihistamines, antidepressants, antiseizure medications, diabetes drugs, heartburn drugs, and others. The list of prescription medications that can cause weight gain runs to fifty or more common drugs. However, a drug that promotes weight gain in one patient may have no effect on another patient's weight or may even promote weight loss in yet another patient. If you have concerns about medication and your weight, talk with your doctor. Often, medications can be adjusted or changed to meet your needs.

WHEN BODY WEIGHT BECOMES A PROBLEM

Using the information and tools in this chapter, you can assess your BMI, waist measurement, and medical history. These three resources together help you determine whether your body is at a healthy weight. If your BMI is between 18.5 and 24.9 *and* your waist measurement is less than 40 inches (for men) or 35 inches (for women) *and* if your medical history raises no red flags, then you are likely to be at a healthy body weight.

If your BMI is 18.5 or lower, you are probably underweight. A low BMI of this sort is often an indication of an eating disorder and should not be dismissed. Evaluation by a medical doctor is essential.

Similarly, if your BMI is 25 or greater, you are likely overweight. If your BMI is 30 or greater, you are probably obese. You may or may not have a family history of weight problems. In either case your weight places you at risk for health problems, and a consultation with your doctor is in order. If you need to lose weight to improve your health, your doctor will help you make a manageable plan to meet your goals.

WHAT TO LOOK FOR IN A
WEIGHT-LOSS PROGRAM

You can get expert help choosing a weight-loss program by talking to a school nurse, a primary care physician, or a registered dietician. You may ask, why go to the trouble of consulting a professional? Health-care providers can help you avoid scams and diet dangers. Before your appointment, it would be a good idea for you to become familiar with some of the weight-loss programs available and write down a list of your questions and concerns. As you gather information, remember that a reputable, reliable weight-loss program includes the following:

- Healthy eating plans that reduce calories but do not rule out specific foods or food groups
- Regular physical activity and/or exercise instruction
- Tips on healthy behavior changes that also consider your cultural needs
- Slow and steady weight loss of about half a pound (.23 kg) to 2 pounds (.91 kg) per week
- Medical supervision if you are planning to follow a special-formula diet, such as a very-low-calorie diet
- A plan to keep the weight off after you have lost It[3]

3
WHAT'S SO IMPORTANT ABOUT BODY WEIGHT?

It doesn't matter how much you weigh as long as you like yourself, right? Not exactly. Body weight does matter when it comes to health, life expectancy, and quality of life. Being measurably overweight increases a person's risk of disease or early death. An estimated 280,000 adults in the United States alone die from health problems associated with obesity each year.[1] When it comes to quality of life, people who are overweight or obese suffer significantly higher rates of depression, low self-esteem, and social difficulties. Body weight, it turns out, is important.

HEALTH RISKS OF OBESITY

Some of the most common health problems associated with obesity are hypertension, stroke, blood cholesterol problems, type 2 diabetes, coronary heart disease, gallbladder disease, osteoarthritis, and respiratory problems. This is quite a list. How exactly do these health problems affect the body?

Hypertension is the medical term for high blood pressure, and about one-third of all obese people suffer from this disease. The American Heart Association explains that "changes in body weight over time and skin fold thickness are related to blood pressure levels. These factors have been linked to the later rise and development of high blood pressure."[2] Some of the possible consequences of high blood pressure are stroke, kidney failure, and heart attack.

A person with hypertension has a greater risk of stroke, also called a "brain attack." A stroke is a sudden loss of brain function. The stroke is caused by a blockage or rupture of a blood vessel to the brain, and the brain suffers a lack of oxygen. Possible symptoms include a loss of muscular control, diminished consciousness, dizziness, slurred speech, and loss of consciousness. The more overweight a person is, the greater his or her risk of stroke.

Another health risk of obesity is problems with blood lipid levels. Obesity is associated with high levels of triglycerides, a form of fat in blood plasma. Excess triglycerides in the blood can lead to coronary artery disease. Obesity is also linked to low levels of HDL cholesterol, the so-called good cholesterol. Scientists believe a high HDL level helps protect against heart attack. A low HDL level indicates an increased risk of heart attack and stroke.

The recommended total cholesterol in people ages two to eighteen is less than 170 mg per 100 ml, but many teens exceed this level. Excess body fat can lead to high levels of triglycerides ("bad" cholesterol) and low levels of HDL cholesterol ("good" cholesterol) in the blood. Children and teens with high cholesterol are at risk of increased cholesterol levels as adults. Associated risks include heart attack and stroke.

Hypertension, stroke, and high lipid levels are risk factors for coronary heart disease. This disease is characterized by blockages in the blood vessels that lead to the heart. Heart attack and death can result. Someone who is overweight has about twice the chance of developing coronary heart disease as a person of a healthy weight. Someone who is obese is over three times as likely to develop coronary heart disease.

The American Diabetes Association warns that type 2 diabetes is associated with obesity, among other risk factors. With this disease the body either does not produce enough insulin or the cells do not respond to insulin properly. Insulin is important to the body because cells need it in order to process sugar, their primary form of energy. When cells do not or cannot use insulin properly, blood glucose levels rise. In response, the pancreas produces even more insulin. The cycle continues as long as the individual is overweight. The cells become starved for energy. Over time, the high glucose levels can cause damage to the eyes, kidneys, nerves, or heart. The longer a person carries excess weight, the greater the risk of developing type 2 diabetes.

Until recent years, type 2 diabetes developed mainly in adults in their forties and older. It was extremely rare in children and adolescents. With the rising occurrence of overweight among people under age twenty, however, type 2 diabetes is on the rise in this age group. With type 2 diabetes, the body suffers an impaired ability to process insulin, and blood glucose levels rise. Complications involve both the circulatory and nervous systems, with specific examples including blindness, kidney failure, heart disease, and amputations.

Most young people diagnosed with the disease are age ten or older, are overweight, and have at least one parent with diabetes. In some cases the young person's diagnosis prompts parents or other relatives to be tested, and only then does an older family member find out that he or she has diabetes, too.

Lifestyle changes that may actually prevent or delay the development of type 2 diabetes include weight management and increased physical activity.

Another health risk of obesity, gallbladder disease, is a

painful inflammation of the gallbladder due to gallstones. In severe cases, the gallbladder can rupture. The person may need surgery to remove the diseased gallbladder. Osteoarthritis, also called degenerative joint disease, occurs typically in older people and people who have been obese for a long time. Excess weight in a person's chest area can cause respiratory problems due to poor respiratory motion and low lung capacity. Some obese persons, including children, suffer sleep apnea syndrome. During the night, the person stops breathing, usually for periods of ten seconds or longer.

All of the health problems and diseases discussed here take time to develop. Experts often stress that risk factors for obesity-related diseases increase over time, and that reducing body weight by even a little can do a lot of good. For these reasons, weight management can be lifesaving. At the very least, achieving and maintaining a healthy weight enriches a person's quality of life.

OBESITY AND QUALITY OF LIFE

A person's quality of life is subjective, meaning that it is a personal assessment by the person and not a judgment by others. To evaluate your own quality of life, you should take into account your physical and mental health as well as how you see your position in your family, social settings, and larger environment—school, job, community.

Quality of life is so important to a person's health and well-being that the World Health Organization (WHO) has devoted a great deal of research and educational resources to the subject. According to WHO:

Quality of life [is] an individual's perception of their position in life in the context of the culture and value systems in which they live and in relation to their goals, expectations, standards and concerns. It is a broad ranging concept affected in a complex way by the person's physical health, psychological state, personal beliefs, social relationships and their relationship to salient [significant] features of their environment.[3]

Being overweight or obese impacts a person's quality of life in many ways. Some of the health risks associated with obesity were outlined in the section above. In obvious ways hypertension, type 2 diabetes, and other diseases contribute to a lower, not a higher, quality of life. Even in the absence of disease, obesity can make life more difficult. Walking up and down stairs, hurrying through hallways to get to class on time, and engaging in active leisure pursuits are more difficult for a person carrying extra weight.

Being overweight or obese can be detrimental to more than just physical health. Studies suggest a link between obesity and depression, especially among younger adolescents, and particularly girls. One possible explanation for this link is that people tend to form opinions of themselves in reaction to how they imagine others see them. Someone who is overweight and senses that others disapprove of or ridicule his or her size is likely to suffer lower self-esteem and poor body image. These negative feelings can contribute to depression.

Depression is characterized by insomnia, weight gain or loss, and feelings of sadness, guilt, apathy, or despair, among other characteristics. Clinical depression is not just "in someone's head." It has very real physical causes. In the brain, chemical messengers called neurotransmitters are responsible for helping to carry messages between nerve cells. When the neurotransmitters that regulate mood are out of synch, depression can result. For instance, the brain's response to a stressful situation or event may alter the balance of neurotransmitters, triggering depression.

Younger adolescents going through puberty experience significant changes in body shape and size at a time when they are extra sensitive to peers' opinions of their bodies. Being overweight or obese at this time in life can be especially distressing. At this age, a smaller percentage of young people are overweight or obese than in high school and beyond. As a result, an overweight middle school student may feel isolated, even ostracized, by his or her excess weight. Depression is one possible result. More common, though, is increased difficulty socializing and fitting in with peers.

According to some studies, girls are more harshly judged according to their weight than are boys.[4] Consequently, girls may be more vulnerable to depression in connection to carrying excess weight. Living in a culture that celebrates thinness as a requirement for beauty and personal worth, an obese girl can easily succumb to feelings of self-rejection and low self-worth. Even without a clinical diagnosis of depression, these feelings, combined with a poor body image, can undermine a person's quality of life. One study found that obese children are over five times more likely to suffer a lower quality of life than children who are not overweight.[5]

A young person—boy or girl—who is overweight and feels social pressure to be thin may resort to dieting. For some people, dieting to gain the approval of others can be even more stressful than being stigmatized for obesity. Eating fewer calories than normal can create a feeling of deprivation, a lack of what's expected. In addition, dieting can bring on feelings of guilt and fear of failure. While dieting to achieve a healthy weight is a good thing with proper guidance, people who diet in direct response to social criticism may only increase their feelings of low self-worth, sadness, and despair.

ARE ANTIFAT ATTITUDES ON THE RISE?

The number of overweight teenagers has nearly tripled in the past two decades.[6] With this rising number, you might expect to see an increasing acceptance of large body sizes. Two researchers, Janet D. Latner and Albert J. Stunkard, set out to determine whether stigmatization of overweight children has increased or decreased since the 1960s, when earlier studies were done. The results of their study may surprise you.

- Since the first studies in the 1960s, bias against overweight young people has increased significantly.
- Obese adolescents in the twelve-to-sixteen-year-old range are frequent victims of aggressive behavior at school.
- When shown drawings of children with a physical disability, excess weight, or no disability, fifth- and sixth-grade students overwhelmingly ranked the obese child last in order of preference.
- First- and second-grade boys assigned negative adjectives such as sloppy and sneaky to pictures of overweight subjects.
- Eighty-six percent of kindergartners expressed an aversion to overweight children.
- When shown drawings of chubby children, children as young as three years old said they would not want to play with those children.

From their study, Latner and Stunkard concluded that antifat attitudes are getting worse. Not only that, but bias against overweight people seems to develop early in life, even before children reach school age. The prejudice appears to get stronger as children get older. These longstanding attitudes can contribute to overweight adolescents' sense of shame, embarrassment, or low self-esteem regarding their appearance.[7]

Obesity does not necessarily lead to depression. Certainly not all obese persons are depressed. Another connection between the two, however, is that depression itself can lead to excess weight gain. Someone who feels unmotivated or unable to eat right and get necessary exercise may gain weight as a result. When food is viewed as a source of solace and comfort in times of depression, the troubled person may eat more or eat more often than normal, resulting in weight gain. The added pounds may trigger feelings of self-rejection, disappointment, or guilt, resulting in deeper depression and yet more eating for comfort.

One eating disorder in particular, binge eating, is associated with the conditions of overweight and obesity. About half of obese binge eaters recall that they first began binging after failed attempts to diet, according to some studies.[8] Binge eating is characterized by frequent episodes of devouring large amounts of food, usually on at least two days a week for six months. The binge episode may occur in a single sitting, such as a two-hour period, during which the person consumes several thousand calories. Gorging does not always occur in distinct episodes, however. Binge eating may occur throughout the day as large meals or nonstop "grazing."

Binge eating was not identified as an eating disorder until the early 1990s, thus research into the disorder is not yet as extensive as studies on some other eating disorders. However, initial findings suggest that the disorder may begin in early childhood. Despite the possibility of early onset, patients with the disorder are typically in the forty-six to fifty-five-year-old range, according to the National Institutes of Health. The disorder afflicts more females than males. Overall, approximately 2 to 3 percent of adolescents and adults are victims of binge eating disorder.[9]

Children and teens who struggle with excess weight are at a greater risk of manifesting eating disorders than their normal-weight peers. One recent study found that overweight boys and girls are more likely to try extreme diets than those who are not overweight.[10] In some young people, extreme dieting is a behavior that advances into a full-fledged eating disorder.

EATING DISORDERS

The three major eating disorders are anorexia nervosa, bulimia nervosa, and binge eating disorder.

Anorexia nervosa

The main characteristics of anorexia are a persistent below-minimal weight, an intense fear of gaining weight/being fat, and distorted body-image. In females a fourth characteristic is amenorrhea (failure to menstruate).

Bulimia nervosa

Bulimia is characterized by repeated episodes of eating large amounts of food, followed by purging behaviors such as forced vomiting or use of laxatives. Excessive exercising to compensate for binge eating is also common.

Binge eating disorder

The primary symptom of binge eating disorder is repeated episodes of gorging large amounts of food, especially when not physically hungry. Unlike bulimics, binge eaters do not purge food or try to make up for binging by exercising excessively. Consequently, binge eaters typically are overweight or obese.

SOME SYMPTOMS OF
BINGE EATING DISORDER

- Repeated episodes of binge eating—usually two days a week or more for six months
- A feeling of lack of control over the eating or inability to stop eating
- Eating much faster than normal during the binge, often too quickly to taste the food
- Eating huge amounts of food when not physically hungry
- Eating alone to hide the amount of food being consumed
- Feelings of guilt, shame, or disgust following the binge
- Overweight or obesity

The main goal of treatment for binge eating disorder is to teach how to eat in response to hunger, not in response to emotions such as depression, loneliness, or anxiety. Patients also learn how to incorporate physical exercise into their lifestyles.

WEIGHT MANAGEMENT
AND QUALITY OF LIFE

When it comes to body weight and health, the best way to maintain a high quality of life is to maintain a healthy weight for your height, year in and year out.

For a person who is already overweight or obese, achieving a healthy weight can lead to better health. For many people, feeling healthier increases their satisfaction with life, especially as previous physical challenges (for example, limited physical agility or respiratory problems) lessen or even disappear.

Losing a significant amount of weight, however, is not a guarantee of instant high self-esteem and stress-free living. Frequently, obese people who lose weight are surprised by changes in social interactions. Friends and family may seem overenthusiastic about the weight loss. People of the opposite sex may show more interest than in the past. While pleased with their healthier bodies, slimmed-down people may feel resentful, annoyed, or even angry that others treat them differently based simply on a decrease in weight. Their smaller body size and the changes in people's attitudes toward them may actually make them feel more vulnerable. Questions of self-worth and self-esteem may rise again to the surface as they adjust not only to changes in their own bodies but to changes in the people around them.

The consequences of being overweight or obese may seem overwhelming. If you have excess weight, don't be discouraged by the information in this chapter. Weight loss, even in small amounts, can reduce your risk of developing health problems. For example, by reducing your body weight by as little as 5 to 10 percent, you can improve your health.[11] Achieving an ideal weight is most healthy and gratifying, but getting started by losing even a little weight has positive results. In the next several chapters, you can learn more about achieving an ideal weight, including facts on nutrition, energy needs, weight-loss plans, and medical interventions that can assist weight loss.

Myth: Being thin makes you happy.
Fact: People of all sizes are happy.
Myth: Fat people tend to be unhappy.
Fact: People of all sizes and weights are unhappy.

4
NUTRITION AND WELLNESS

Good nutrition contributes to your overall wellness, the combined goal of your physical and mental health. Poor nutrition, which can occur with or without obesity, breaks down not only your body's wellness but your psychological wellness, too.

The body is designed to thrive on healthful foods. In particular, the digestive process ensures that nutrients in foods and drinks are processed and used throughout the body. Knowing how the body processes food may help you to understand your body's need for good nutrition. It may also help you recognize the damages caused by eating too much or too little.

The moment food or drink enters your mouth, your body begins to extract nutrition. As you chew, glands in the mouth produce saliva that breaks down starches into smaller particles. When you swallow, the food passes through the esophagus to the stomach, where foods and liquids are mixed with digestive juices that further disintegrate food particles. Then, the partially digested matter empties into the small intestine, where juices from the intestine, the pancreas, and the liver continue the process. Finally, the digested molecules of food, along with water and minerals, are absorbed through the intestine walls. They are carried by the bloodstream through-out the body for storage or further processing, depending on the nutrient. Waste matter (such as fiber and cells shed from intestinal walls) is formed in the large intestine and then is pushed into the colon and expelled as feces.

THE DIGESTIVE SYSTEM

Mouth and salivary glands

Esophagus

Liver

Stomach Pancreas

Gallbladder

Duodenum

Transverse colon

Descending colon

Ascending colon

Jejunum

Cecum

Small Intestine

Ileum

Appendix

Sigmoid colon

Rectum

Anus

The complex digestive system breaks down food so that it is usable by the body.

The digestive process breaks food into components that are used for energy, for body structures (bones, muscles, and body fat), and for regulation of body functions (for example, the control of body temperature and chemical reactions). Though the body needs more than forty nutrients to stay alive and healthy, nutrition doesn't have to be complicated. Numerous books are available on the subject, and you can plan your own nutrition by understanding a few key concepts and using a daily eating guide such as MyPyramid, the revised and updated version of the USDA food guide pyramid. These concepts are discussed in this and the following chapter.

THE SIX CLASSES OF NUTRIENTS

The forty-plus nutrients the body needs to survive are grouped into six classes: carbohydrates, protein, lipids (fats), vitamins, minerals, and water.

Carbohydrates

Carbohydrates include sugars, starches, and most fibers. Foods rich in carbohydrates include cereals, grains, vegetables, pasta, potatoes, and sugary foods and drinks. Most carbohydrates—the sugars and the starches—are converted by the body into glucose, an energy source for the body. While fiber is not usable as energy, it is important to the health of the digestive tract. Fiber is found in whole grains, vegetables, fruits, and legumes (peas, beans, and lentils).

Carbohydrates occur in two forms: simple and complex. *Simple carbohydrates* include the naturally occurring sugar in fruit called fructose. Simple carbohydrates also include the sugars in syrups, honey, and sucrose, the white processed sugar used in baked goods and sweetened beverages. Simple carbohydrates are sources of quick energy because they are easily converted to glucose and rapidly enter the bloodstream.

Complex carbohydrates, found in most grain products, vegetables, and potatoes, are digested more slowly. They provide energy over a longer period of time.

Protein

Protein is formed of chains of amino acids. The body uses amino acids to make its own unique proteins, which it uses for the growth and repair of tissues such as muscle, bone, cartilage, and teeth. Amino acids also help regulate such vital bodily functions as carrying oxygen to cells and fighting infection. When carbohydrates are unavailable, protein can be converted to glucose for energy. High-protein foods include eggs, milk, meat, fish, and poultry, as well as certain vegetables, grains, and beans.

Lipids

Lipids (fats) are present in foods derived from both animals and plants. Like carbohydrates, lipids are a good source of energy. The body also needs fats for cell membrane structure, for blood-clotting functions, and to transport the fat-soluble vitamins A, D, E, and K throughout the body.

Triglycerides are the main components of fat. When we talk about the fat content of a food, we are talking about triglycerides. Triglycerides are made up of three fatty acids and glycerol. Depending on how the fatty acids and glycerol are combined, the fat may be saturated or unsaturated. *Saturated fats* are solid at room temperature. Think of a stick of butter or the veins of fat in a raw steak. *Unsaturated fats* are liquid at room temperature. Unsaturated fats are found in cooking oils and nonliquid foods such as nuts, olives, and fish.

Vitamins

Vitamins are organic substances found in tiny amounts in plant and animal foods. Although vitamins do not provide

All fats provide 9 calories per gram, but all fats are not equally beneficial. Here are several different kinds of fats that you will find in foods. The first one listed, monounsaturated fat, is considered the most healthful, while trans fat, listed last, is least healthful.

Monounsaturated fat This fat is liquid at room temperature but may become cloudy or semisolid in the refrigerator. You'll find it in olive, canola, and nut oils as well as in avocadoes, almonds, cashews, and other nuts. This fat is considered good because it helps to lower blood cholesterol.

Polyunsaturated fat This fat is liquid or soft at room temperature and in the refrigerator. You'll find it in vegetable oils, pecans, and cold-water fish such as salmon. Although this fat can help lower blood cholesterol levels, the process of lowering cholesterol can be restrained by certain other chemical processes in the body.

Saturated fat This fat is usually solid or waxy at room temperature. It is found in red meats, dairy products, and tropical oils such as coconut and palm oils. This kind of fat can raise blood cholesterol levels and increase your risk of coronary artery disease.

Trans fat This fat is sometimes called partially hydrogenated vegetable oil. It is considered a bad fat because it raises blood cholesterol levels. You'll find it in shortening and most margarines, and in foods prepared with them, such as cookies and crackers.

energy, they are vital to the body's metabolic processes that yield energy. The body also uses vitamins to maintain the health of eyes and bones. Still other vitamins play roles in blood clotting and in tissue growth and development. Antioxidants, such as vitamin E, protect against free radicals, by-products of oxidation in cells that can damage or destroy cells.

Some vitamins are water-soluble and others are fat-soluble. This means that some are carried within the body by water and some are carried by fat. The B-complex vitamins and vitamin C are water-soluble, while vitamins A, D, E, and K are fat-soluble.

Minerals

In contrast to vitamins, which are organic substances, minerals are inorganic (they do not contain carbon). Plants obtain minerals from soil and water, animals obtain minerals by eating plants and drinking water, and humans obtain minerals by eating plants and animals. Like vitamins, minerals do not provide energy but are essential to life-sustaining bodily processes. Some minerals are vital to the structures of bones, teeth, and muscles. Others are necessary for enzymes to function, enabling chemical reactions in the body. Still others, called electrolytes, help to balance fluids in the body and help to regulate the acid-base content of the blood.

Water

An adult's body is made up of 50 to 65 percent water. An infant's body is 70 to 85 percent water.[1] Without taking in water, the human body can survive only a few days. Nearly every chemical reaction within the body uses water. Water is also crucial to digestion, the absorption and transport of nutrients, the growth and repair of tissues, and the removal of waste through urine. Water also helps regulate body temperature and maintain body structure. To include water in your diet, you can drink plain water, drink water mixed into other beverages, or eat foods containing water, such as fruits and vegetables.

A NUTRITIOUS DIET

The body needs nutrients in varying amounts. For instance, protein and carbohydrates are needed in greater amounts than vitamins and minerals. A nutritious diet includes the right balance of nutrients for your body, taking into account your gender, age, level of physical activity, and other factors such as illness or pregnancy.

To determine the amounts of nutrients you need daily, you can consult the Dietary Reference Intakes (DRIs) charts created by the Food and Nutrition Board of the National Academy of Sciences. In the back of this book are the full charts, created for people of all ages. The chart in this chapter shows DRIs for teenagers.

Reading the nutrition facts label on foods and beverages will inform you of the specific nutrients you are consuming. These labels can help you plan your meals to include the ideal amounts of nutrition and energy to meet your daily needs. The Federal Drug Administration (FDA) requires nutrition facts labels on all regulated food products. The few exceptions include very tiny packages and fast food. To ensure reliability and accuracy, all food packagers must use the same format for the nutrition facts label. A label always lists information for one normal-sized serving of the food or drink. For example, a manufacturer cannot list an absurdly small serving size of a food to make it seem low-calorie.

DIETARY REFERENCE INTAKES
FOR TEENAGERS

	MALES AGES 14–19	FEMALES AGES 14–19
Total water (8-ounce cup)	14–15	10–11
Carbohydrate (gram)	130	130
Protein (gram)	52–56	46
Vitamin A (microgram)	625–630	485–500
Vitamin C (milligram)	63–75	56–60
Vitamin E (milligram)	12	12
Thiamin (milligram)	1.0	0.9
Riboflavin (milligram)	1.1	0.9
Niacin (milligram)	12	11
Vitamin B6 (milligram)	1.1	1.0–1.1
Folate (microgram)	320–330	320–330
Vitamin B12 (microgram)	2.0	2.0
Copper (microgram)	685–700	685–700
Iodine (microgram)	95	95
Iron (milligram)	6.0–7.7	7.9–8.1
Magnesium (milligram)	330–340	255–300
Molybdenum (microgram)	33–34	33–34
Phosphorus (milligram)	1,055 (ages 14–18)	1,055 (ages 14–18)
	580 (age 19)	580 (age 19)
Selenium (microgram)	45	45
Zinc (milligram)	8.5–9.4	6.8–7.3

* Total water includes all water consumed through food, beverages, and drinking water. Source: Adapted from Food and Nutrition Board, The National Academy of Sciences.

Here is a sample label for a single-serving container of apricot-mango-flavored yogurt.

The "% Daily Value" numbers (sometimes written % DV) help you judge how much of your daily needs are met by this product. For a 2,000-calorie diet, for example, the container of yogurt provides 25 percent of your calcium needs for the day—a significant amount. On the other hand, the yogurt provides only 6 percent of the vitamin C for the day. Using this information, you could balance this snack by drinking a few ounces of citrus juice to get additional vitamin C.

Nutrition Facts

Serving Size 1 container (170g)
Servings Per Container 1

Amount Per Serving

Calories 160

Calories from Fat 15

	%
Daily Values*	
Total Fat 2g	3%
Saturated Fat 1g	5%
Trans Fat 0g	
Cholesterol 10mg	3%
Sodium 110mg	5%
Total Carbohydrate 30g	10%
Dietary Fiber 2g	8%
Sugars 29g	
Protein 7g	
Vitamin A	8%
Vitamin C	6%
Calcium	25%
Iron	4%

* Percent Daily Values are based on a 2,000-calorie diet. Your daily values may be higher or lower depending on your calorie needs.

Calories:	2,000	2,500
Total Fat	Less than 65g	80g
Sat Fat	Less than 20g	25g
Cholesterol	Less than 300mg	300mg
Sodium	Less than 2,400mg	
	2,400mg	
Total Carbohydrate	300g	375g
Dietary Fiber	25g	30g

Knowing the nutrient content of foods helps you to eat healthfully, which in turn helps you manage your weight. How? This knowledge allows you to select nutrient-dense foods instead of "fluff" foods containing little nutritional value. As a result, you will nourish yourself with necessary nutrients without packing in empty calories. In the following chapter, you will learn more about selecting foods that make up a nutritious diet tailored to your personal energy needs.

5
HOW MUCH SHOULD YOU EAT?

You learned in chapter 1 that weight management is the act of balancing energy intake versus output. To remain at a steady weight, you must consume about the same number of calories per day on average, as your body needs to function for the day. This amount varies from person to person, depending on age, gender, size, and level of activity. Not all people need to just maintain their weight at the current level. Depending upon a person's body mass index, he or she may need to lose weight. Doing so means creating an imbalance in energy intake versus output by expending more energy than is consumed. Conversely, someone who is underweight may need to gain weight to reach optimal health.

ENERGY SOURCES

The energy your body uses comes from two sources: the foods and beverages you consume and the energy stored in your body.

To measure the energy in foods and beverages, we use the kilocalorie, or as it is commonly called, the calorie. A scientist will tell you that 1 calorie is the quantity of heat energy required to raise the temperature of 1 gram of water by

1 degree Celsius at 1 atmospheric pressure. The calorie content of each type of nutrient varies. Fat provides the most calories: 9 calories per gram of fat. Carbohydrates and protein each provide 4 calories per gram. Take a look at the chart showing calorie contents of some common foods and beverages.

CALORIE CONTENTS OF SOME COMMON FOODS AND BEVERAGES

Food or beverage	Serving size	Calories*
Water	8 oz	0
Milk, whole	8 oz	150
Milk, fat-free	8 oz	90
Soda, regular	12 oz	150
Pasta, boiled	1 cup	160
Broccoli, raw	1 cup	24
Bread, whole wheat	1 slice	61
Cheese, cheddar	1 oz	114
Egg, chicken	1	79
Chocolate candy bar	1.65 oz	136–260
Butter	1 teaspoon	36
Apple	1 medium	81
Beef, lean, ground, sautéed	3.5 oz	275
Chicken, white meat without skin, roasted	3.5 oz	173

*Average calories. Values for specific foods or beverages may vary. Check the label.

Source: Adapted from Kirschmannm, Gayla J., and John D. Kirschmann, "Table of Food Composition," *Nutrition Almanac*, 4th edition (New York: McGraw-Hill, 1996), pp. 389–469; and Hensrud, Donald D., editor, "Dietician's Tips," *Mayo Clinic: Healthy Weight for Everybody* (Rochester, MN: Mayo Clinic Health Information, 2005), p. 297.

See the Metric Conversion Chart on page 98 for metric equivalents of these measurements.

The chart lists calories found in individual foods. Often, however, you eat soups, salads, sandwiches, entrées, and other dishes made up of several foods. To get the total calorie count of a mixed-ingredient dish, you could add up the calories contributed by each ingredient. For example, suppose you make a grilled cheese sandwich using 2 slices of whole wheat bread, 2 teaspoons (10 ml) of butter, and 1 ounce (28 g) of cheddar cheese. That sandwich has a total of 308 calories. For prepackaged foods, you can consult the nutrition facts label on the package that lists the calories and nutrients per serving. For instance, the label on a box of typical whole grain oat cereal says that 1 cup (227 g) of cereal with half a cup (118 ml) of fat-free milk has a total of 150 calories.

Another source of energy for your body is its own stores of glycogen and fat. After you eat a meal containing carbohydrates, glucose is absorbed into the blood. This causes a release of insulin, which signals body tissues, especially muscles and liver, to take in, store, and use the glucose. If some or all of the glucose is not needed immediately for energy, the glucose is stored, mostly as glycogen. This process is called glycogenesis. Later, when the body needs energy, it can break down the glycogen into glucose again. This process is called glycogenolysis. The body usually stores just enough glycogen to supply energy needs for twelve to twenty-four hours. Additional glucose may be stored as fat.

After a meal containing lipids (fats), the body stores excess energy as fat. Fat is stored in the form of triglycerides. Most triglycerides are in adipose tissue. These tissues are made up of adipocytes, or fat cells. As triglycerides fill the fat cells, the cells get bigger, like tiny balloons. You may be interested to know that most fat cells in a person's body are formed during infancy and adolescence. Once you reach adulthood, only excessive weight gain can cause your body to form new fat cells. The more fat cells your body has, the greater its ability to store triglycerides, or fat.

In the hours after you have eaten, your body can break down triglycerides into glycerol and fatty acids, which can be used to produce energy. Between meals, the body uses some of its supply of glycogen and triglycerides for energy. At the next meal the body replaces these energy stores. This sort of eating pattern creates a balance of energy intake versus output. An energy deficit is created when you consume less energy than your body needs. Then it uses stored energy without being able to replace it. As a result, your body weight decreases. You will lose 1 pound (.45 kg) of body fat for every 3,500 calories that are used but not replaced in energy stores.

HOW MUCH ENERGY DOES YOUR BODY NEED DAILY?

To get an idea of how many calories you need per day, simply to stay alive and healthy, consider four factors: age, sex, body size and composition, and level of physical activity.

Age

Children and adolescents, whose bodies are still growing, need more energy to function daily than adults do. They are still developing bones, muscles, and tissues. During puberty, a young person's body grows and develops rapidly, including a period known as a growth spurt. During the growth spurt, which typically unfolds over two to three years, a girl grows several inches taller—3 inches (8 cm) is common—and gains from 10 to 30 pounds (4.5 to 13 kg). A boy's growth spurt may result in a gain of up to 8 inches (20 cm) or more in height with a corresponding gain in weight—perhaps 10 or more pounds (4.5 kg or more) in a year.

Once people reach adulthood and begin to age, their bodies need less energy per pound to function and remain healthy. An adult's resting metabolic rate (RMR) is lower than a teenager's. Generally, an adult's RMR and energy needs lessen by about 2 percent every decade.

Sex

Your sex can make a difference in your daily energy needs. Typically, males who have gone through puberty have less body fat and more muscle than females of the same age and weight. More muscle results in a higher RMR and higher energy requirements.

Body size and composition

As a general rule, a larger body requires more energy to function than a smaller body. Regarding the body's composition, muscle burns more calories than body fat does, so a muscled body needs more energy daily than a similar-sized body with less muscle.

Physical activity increases the body's needs for energy and water.

Level of physical activity

Your level of physical activity directly affects your daily energy requirements. Basically, the more active you are, the more energy your body will demand. When determining daily calorie needs, medical experts consider whether a person's lifestyle is sedentary, moderately active, or active. If you lead a sedentary lifestyle, you are sitting for most of the day. For example, sitting at a desk most of the day, whether at school or in an office, is sedentary. If you lead a moderately active lifestyle, you include daily activities that involve standing and walking. Typical activities include teaching,

RECOMMENDED DAILY CALORIE INTAKES FOR INDIVIDUALS AT DIFFERENT LEVELS OF PHYSICAL ACTIVITY

Gender	Age (in years)	Sedentary	Moderately Active	Active
Child	2-3	1,000	1,000-1,400	1,000-1,400
Female	4-8	1,200	1,400-1,600	1,400-1,800
	9-13	1,600	1,600-2,000	1,800-2,200
	14-18	1,800	2,000	2,4000
	19-30	2,000	2,000-2,200	2,400
	31-50	1,800	2,000	2,200
	51+	1,600	1,800	2,000-2,200
Male	4-8	1,400	1,400-1,600	1,600-2,000
	9-13	1,800	1,800-2,200	2,000-2,600
	14-18	2,200	2,400-2,800	2,800-3,200
	19-30	2,400	2,600-2,800	3,000
	31-50	2,200	2,400-2,600	2,800-3,000
	51+	2,000	2,200-2,400	2,400-2,800

yard work, traveling by foot, and working in a job that calls for standing or walking, such as retail sales or waiting tables. If you lead an active lifestyle, you include daily activities that involve exertion and tend to raise the body's temperature. Examples include dancing, playing sports, and jobs that require manual labor such as construction work or farming.

See the chart below listing recommended energy requirements for people of different ages, sexes, and activity levels. As you can see from the recommended daily intake chart, being physically active boosts your body's use of energy, or calories.

CALORIE/ ENERGY USE IN PERSONS OF DIFFERENT WEIGHTS

Activity (1 hour)	130 lbs.	155 lbs.	190 lbs.
Bicycling, less than 10 mph, leisure	236	281	345
Bicycling, 12-13.9 mph, moderate effort	472	563	690
Bowling	177	211	259
Calisthenics (pushups, sit-ups), vigorous effort	472	563	690
Dancing, aerobic, ballet or modern, twist	354	422	518
Rope jumping, moderate effort	590	704	863
Running in place	472	563	690
Running, 6 mph	590	704	863
Running, 10 mph	944	1126	1380
Swimming laps, freestyle, light/moderate effort	472	563	690
Swimming laps, freestyle, fast, vigorous effort	590	704	863
Tennis, doubles	354	422	518
Tennis, singles	472	563	690
Walking, 2 mph, slow pace	148	176	216
Walking, 4 mph, very brisk pace	236	281	345

Source: Adapted from NutriStrategy, "Calories Burned During Exercise."
http://www.nutristrategy.com/activitylist4.htm (accessed 9-19-06).

The chart on calorie/energy use (page 55) shows approximately how many calories are used in various activities by 150-(68-kg), 200-(91-kg), and 250-pound (113-kg) persons.

PLANNING YOUR MEALS

To set up your daily eating plan, use a guide that recommends numbers of servings in each of the different food groups. The U.S. Department of Agriculture developed a visual guide for daily eating called MyPyramid. As you can see

in the illustration, MyPyramid uses bands of different colors to represent the five major food groups plus oils. A healthy diet includes foods from all six groups every day.

The bands on the pyramid are different widths to show relative proportions of each food group. Notice that the widest band is grains. Your daily diet should include more grain products than any other foods. The bands for vegetables and milk are about the same size. Include each of these food groups in amounts slightly smaller than grains. Fruits and meat and beans are proportionately smaller, so include these foods in lesser amounts. The slimmest band is oils; include only a little oil in your daily diet. On the left side of the pyramid, the figure climbing steps is a reminder to stay physically active along with eating nutritiously.

In the pyramid, the *grains* group includes foods made from wheat, rice, oats, cornmeal, and barley. In general, a 1-ounce (28 gram) serving is 1 slice of bread, 1 cup (227 g) of breakfast cereal, or half a cup (113 g) of cooked rice, pasta, or oatmeal.

The *vegetables* group includes both vegetables and vegetable juices. A normal serving from this group is, for example, 1 cup (227 g) of raw or cooked vegetables, 1 cup (240 ml) of vegetable juice, or 2 cups (454 g) of raw leafy greens.

The *fruits* group includes fruits and fruit juices. A serving is, in general, 1 cup of fruit (227 ml) or fruit juice (240 ml) or half a cup (113 g) of dried fruit.

The *oils* group includes butter and liquid oils, such as corn oil and olive oil, as well as the oils found in nuts, fish, avocadoes, mayonnaise, salad dressings, margarine, and other foods.

The *milk* group includes all milk and milk products that retain their calcium content. For example, yogurt is part of the milk group, but butter—a milk product—is part of the oils group. A serving in this group is, for example, 1 cup (240 ml) of milk or yogurt, one-and-a-half ounces (43 g) of natural cheese (such as cheddar or swiss), or 2 ounces (57 g) of processed cheese (such as Velveeta, American, or Cheez Whiz).

The *meat and beans* group contains a variety of protein-rich foods. A 1-ounce (28 g) serving in this group is the equivalent of, for example, 1 ounce (28 g) of lean meat, poultry, or

RECOMMENDED DAILY FOOD INTAKES FOR TEENAGERS

CALORIE LEVEL	2,000	2,200	2,400	2,600	2,800
Grains	6 oz	7 oz	8 oz	9 oz	10 oz
Vegetables	2.5 cups	3 cups	3 cups	3.5 cups	3.5 cups
Fruits	2 cups	2 cups	2 cups	2 cups	2.5 cups
Oils	6 tsp	6 tsp	7 tsp	8 tsp	8 tsp
Milk	3 cups	3 cups	3 cups	3 cups	3 cups
Meat and Beans	5.5 oz	6 oz	6.5 oz	6.5 oz	7 oz
Discretionary calorie allowance*	267	290	362	410	426

* The discretionary calorie allowance is the number of calories left over after accounting for th foods listed in the column above it. The individual should choose additional foods, according preference, to meet this allowance.
Source: Adapted from United States Department of Agriculture, "MyPyramid: Food Inta Patterns."
See the Metric Conversion Chart on page 98 for metric equivalents of these measurements

fish; one-quarter cup (57 g) dried beans, cooked; 1 egg; 1 tablespoon (15 ml) of peanut butter; or half an ounce (14 g) of nuts or seeds.

Most teenagers need 2,000-2,800 calories a day to supply their energy needs. The recommended daily food chart (above) lists daily amounts of each food group, plus oils/fats, to meet these energy needs.

At first using guides such as the dietary reference intakes and MyPyramid may take a little effort. Once you develop a sense of what kinds of foods and portions make up a healthy diet, however, you can create nutritious meals and snacks on your own. Learning how to meet your own nutrition needs in this way boosts your overall well-being. Your knowledge of basic nutrition not only helps you to stay healthy, it also helps you to manage your weight. In the next chapter, you will learn more about managing your weight, including setting goals, identifying challenges, sticking to meal plans, and being physically active.

Myth: Skipping meals helps you lose weight.
Fact: Skipping meals can lead to strong, even overwhelming, feelings of hunger and, as a result, overeating.

6
ROAD MAP TO A HEALTHY WEIGHT

Chances are, if you are overweight, this book is not the first resource you've consulted for information on weight loss or weight management. You may have read some of the scores of magazine articles and books promising just the right diet (low-carb, high-protein, low-fat, grapefruit, cabbage, powders, bars, supplements—you name it). You may have attempted to lose weight before and judged your success or failure by the numbers on the bathroom scales. For many people, reaching a healthy weight can seem overwhelming. Where do you start? How do you proceed? What constitutes success? What if you never make it to model-thin? If you can't reach an ideal weight and maintain it, should you try to lose weight at all?

The truth is, weight management and your health are about a great deal more than just how much you weigh. They are about more than lists of "good" foods and "bad" foods, too. Weight management and health certainly do not hinge on fad diets or remarkable pills sold at discounts over the Internet. Most definitely, success is measured in small steps that you can achieve.

So what is a realistic road map to a healthy weight for you? Experts urge people who are overweight or obese to focus on improving their health through lifestyle changes, not on reaching a specific number on the scales. These lifestyle changes include three basic goals: *reducing your energy intake, increasing your energy output*, and *making changes in your behaviors to prevent weight gain*. In short, weight management should be long-term and sustainable. Even if you do not reach your ideal weight, the weight that you do lose, and keep off, lessens your health risks and enriches your quality of life.

MAKING A PLAN AND SETTING GOALS

To get started making your own weight-management plan, ask yourself a few questions.

Where am I in terms of childhood or adolescent growth and development? With people whose bodies are still developing, care must be taken to not interrupt the growth process by restricting nutrient and energy intake. For many young people, the best plan is to maintain a steady weight while allowing their bodies to "catch up" to the weight by growing taller and increasing muscle mass. A pediatrician (a doctor who specializes in children and adolescents) or a family physician can be a great help in setting weight-management goals for young people.

What is a realistic weight-loss goal for me? Start by thinking of just the next six months. In that time period, a 5 to 10 percent reduction in body weight is reasonable for adults. To see healthy ranges of heights and weights, you can look back at the charts in chapter 2.

Let's say you stand 5' 7" (170 cm) tall and weigh 185 pounds (84 kg). For your height, a weight of around 155 (70 kg) or less is desirable. You don't need to lose all 30 pounds (14 kg) in six months, however, or even in a year. If you lost 10 percent of 185 pounds in six months, that would be an 18.5-pound loss. A 5 percent loss would be about 9 pounds (4 kg). This rate of loss amounts to less than a pound a week. Experts recommend losing no more than 2 pounds (1 kg) a week. Remember, if your body is still growing, your needs may be different, so consult your doctor.

What behaviors do I need to change? Changing your behaviors to encourage weight loss or weight management includes making lists of dos and don'ts. (An example is on page 64.) The idea is to try out and adapt to behaviors that promote healthy eating and exercising, while slowly eliminating behaviors that promote weight gain. As with your weight-loss goals, approach these goals at a reasonable rate. For instance, begin by brainstorming for a list of *all* the dos and don'ts that you can think of. Then circle just three in each category to work on in the next six months. Save the list for future reference.

To keep track of your goals and progress, a weight-management diary or calendar is useful. Record information such as what and when you eat, how you feel when you eat (hungry, bored, guilty, etc.), when and how long you exercise, and other comments that may motivate you and help you to track progress. Decide ahead of time how often you will weigh yourself, and limit weigh-ins to those days only. Remember that weight management is about achieving health and well-being, not about obsessing over the bathroom scales.

Above all, make sure that your weight-loss plan and goals are *realistic* and *attainable*. If you are not a morning person, it's unrealistic to plan to get up at 5:00 AM every day to exercise. This plan will likely lead to frustration and failure. Why not work with your natural body rhythms and work out in the afternoon or evening? If you hate the taste of broccoli or salmon, plan meals that don't include these foods. Eat foods you like, and try out new ones occasionally to expand your options. There's a whole universe of interesting and healthful foods out there.

Suggestions for Behavioral Changes to Promote Weight Loss

Do

- Set a pattern of regular meals and snacks.
- Eat smaller portion sizes.
- Limit second helpings to vegetables and fruit.
- Drink more water.
- Choose low-fat dairy products.
- Use healthy cooking methods, such as baking, steaming, and microwaving to replace frying.
- Be physically active for thirty minutes or more on most days of the week.

Don't

- Drink sugary beverages, such as soda, that have little or no nutritional value.
- Compare your weight to your friends' weights.
- Park yourself in front of a television, computer, or video game in your spare time.
- Clean your plate just to avoid wasting food.
- Splurge by treating yourself to huge restaurant or fast food meals.
- Eat in response to emotions such as boredom, sadness, or anxiety.
- Reward yourself with food.

To make sure that goals are attainable, think "little steps." If you have never undertaken an exercise program before, don't expect to jog a mile the first day. Instead, set attainable goals such as walking fifteen minutes a day for the first week, or walking once around a quarter-mile track each day. The next week, increase your walking time to twenty minutes a day or one-and-a-half times around the track. Likewise, don't ban a favorite food from your diet completely. The key is in not overdoing it. An occasional cupcake is reasonable, for example, but not two or three of them at one sitting.

Make sure your maximum workout goal is attainable, too. Perhaps this is walking thirty minutes five days a week, or walking two or three times around the track each day. You don't have to be a marathon runner or a weight-lifting champion to lose weight and stay fit. The idea is to reach a goal you have set and stick with it, not to keep adding on to the goal every time you get close to attaining it.

STICKING WITH YOUR MEAL PLANS

In chapters 4 and 5, you learned about nutrition, the food guide pyramid, and planning meals. Your road map to a healthy weight includes sticking with the plans you made for nutritious meals and snacks.

When you eat at home, you must have a properly stocked pantry and refrigerator in order to implement your meal plans. It's one thing to plan a daily breakfast that includes fresh fruit. It's another thing to actually have the fruit on hand each morning. If you don't do the shopping at your house, discuss your meal plans with the person who does. Make handy shopping lists for this person and offer positive feedback when the foods you need show up in the kitchen.

Having healthy foods at home makes a nutritious diet convenient.

You can cook meats and vegetables without a lot of fat. Here are some ways of preparing foods the low-fat way.

Bake it. Cook food in the oven. For example, bake potatoes and chicken parts with seasonings instead of frying them.

Braise it. First, brown the food, then simmer it in a pan with a small amount of liquid. For example, brown a roast in a small amount of hot oil to seal in its juices, then simmer it in broth in a covered pot.

Broil it. Use the broiling unit of an oven. Broiling works best with medium, not thick, cuts of meats, fish, and vegetables.

Grill it. Cook food using the direct heat of hot coals. For example, grill skewered vegetables, corn on the cob, and hamburgers.

Microwave it. Microwave food, covered, with just a tiny amount of water if necessary. This method works great for fresh or frozen vegetables. For any food, it preserves more vitamins and nutrients than many other cooking methods.

Poach it. Place food in simmering (not boiling) liquid such as water (for eggs) or broth (for fish, chicken, sliced vegetables).

Roast it. Roasting is a lot like baking except at a higher temperature. Cook the food, covered or uncovered, in the oven. Roasting works well with larger cuts of meat, whole poultry, and most vegetables.

Sauté it. Cook chopped or thinly sliced foods quickly in a small amount of oil, broth, or cooking spray.

Steam it. Place the food in a slotted basket or sieve over a pan with shallow boiling water in it. Hot steam cooks the food while keeping it moist. This method is great for fish (add a little lemon juice to the boiling water) and vegetables.

Stir-fry it. Cook chopped-up or thinly sliced meats and vegetables in a small amount of oil over high heat, stirring frequently.

Unless you live alone, you will share many meals with other people in your house. Talk with the person who normally cooks and explain the kinds of foods you need— vegetables, grains, meats or other protein sources, and so forth. Make menu suggestions, too. For instance, vegetables can be added to soups, pizzas, casseroles, omelets, sandwiches, stir-frys, even hamburger patties (try shredded carrots or zucchini mixed into the ground beef).

Volunteer to cook some meals yourself. It is the perfect opportunity to introduce your family to a new way of eating. As well, preparing healthful meals demonstrates how important your eating plan is to you. Gaining the understanding and support of family members can be a big help in sticking to your plans and meeting your goals.Another challenge to your healthy meal plans is dessert. Should you cut out dessert completely? Should you ban chocolate from your lips? And speaking of sweets, is maple syrup on your waffle a bad thing?

The key to desserts and sweets is moderation, not banishment. Prohibiting your favorite treats entirely can lead to feelings of frustration and discouragement. Instead, plan ahead to include reasonable amounts of sweets. Decide ahead of time how much of any of them you will eat and then stop there. To balance the intake of extra energy, you may decide to increase your physical activity that day.

You can also experiment with the preparation of treats to decrease the amount of sugar and fat you consume. Examples include substituting some of the oil in a recipe with applesauce, reducing the amount of sugar in a recipe, and topping your waffle with yogurt instead of syrup. You can also experiment with new kinds of desserts. Try an apple baked with cinnamon and a dollop of butter instead of a slice of apple pie.

As you begin to put your healthy meal and snack plans into action, pay attention to portion sizes. It is helpful to use measuring cups or spoons or a small scale to help serve a recommended amount. Using a smaller plate helps put things into perspective. Smaller portions do not have to be less satisfying. To pump up the satisfaction level, take smaller bites. You'll find that a small bite provides as much taste as a large bite, plus you get more bites.

Portion Sizes
Visualize familiar objects to help you remember portion sizes.

- Deck of cards: 3 ounces (85 g) of meat, poultry, or fish
- Pair of dice: 1.5 ounces (43 g) of hard cheese
- Tennis ball: 1 ounce (28 g) of dry breakfast cereal
- Computer mouse: 1 medium potato
- Compact disc: 1 pancake
- Your thumb tip: 1 teaspoon (5 ml) of butter or mayonnaise
- Your fist: 1 medium piece of fresh fruit

To boost satisfaction with your new, smaller meals, focus on the food and not on the television, a phone conversation, your homework, or some other distraction. It's hard to feel satisfied when you barely remember eating.

What if you eat the meal you planned but still feel hungry? Keep in mind that it may take up to half an hour for your body to register the meal and feel full. (This is a good reason for eating slowly.) If you eat slowly but a meal still leaves you feeling hungry, serve yourself a predetermined food to fill yourself up, such as fresh vegetable sticks or a few wheat crackers.

If you are regularly hungry after meals, ask yourself if you are reducing your food intake too much too soon. Give your body and mind a chance to adjust to changes at a realistic rate.

STAYING PHYSICALLY ACTIVE

Besides sticking with your meal plans, staying physically active is key to weight loss and weight management. If you are not used to exercising, you may feel challenged as you try to establish a routine. Finding activities that you enjoy, choosing appropriate clothes and equipment, and preventing injury are all part of the picture.

For any activity, plan your workout in three stages: warm-up, exercise, and cooldown. The warm-up prepares your body for what's to follow. Get your muscles warm and flexible by stretching, marching in place, or walking slowly. The exercise itself should make you breathe harder, working your lungs and muscles; it also raises your body temperature and heart rate. Weight-bearing activities involve lifting weights or using your own body as a weight (think of using dumbbells or doing push-ups). Non-weight-bearing activities involve actions that put less stress on your joints (think of swimming and biking). The cooldown helps your body return to a normal temperature and rate of breathing. If you are walking or biking, for example, begin slowing down little by little. If you are lifting weights, finish by slowly stretching the muscles you worked.

Even if you are overweight or obese now, plenty of exercises exist that you can enjoy without injury. The exercise chart lists a few ideas beyond traditional team sports. For most of them, you do not need special skills, professional training, or expensive equipment. To make exercising fun, you can do any of these workouts with a friend or join a class.

With any type of exercise program, be alert to warning signs that you need to slow down or stop. These include shortness of breath, rapid heartbeat, muscle cramps, dizziness, and

69

EXERCISES TO INCREASE YOUR LEVEL OF PHYSICAL ACTIVITY

Activity	Explanation	Tips
Walking or Running	A weight-bearing activity. Regular sessions of steady walking or running that make you breathe more heavily are ideal. Build your endurance slowly, starting with 5 or 10 minutes a day and building up to longer sessions.	Wear comfortable shoes with absorbent socks. Before using a treadmill, check its weight-bearing limit; start with a pace of 2 mph.
Dancing	Dancing on your feet is a weight-bearing activity. Dancing while seated—moving just arms and legs—is a non-weight-bearing activity.	Wear clothes that make you feel comfortable. Avoid high-heeled or slick-soled shoes. You can dance alone, with a partner, or in a group.
Water workouts	Water exercises are non-weight-bearing. They help you improve flexibility and increase strength, and they reduce your risk of sore muscles, sore joints, and injuries.	Nonswimmers can try shallow-water workouts. A local YMCA, health club, or school club may offer classes.
Weight training	This is a weight-bearing activity that strengthens your bones and tones and builds muscle. Start with an amount of weight that you can lift six times in a row. Once you can easily lift it fifteen times in a row, move up to a higher weight.	Proper form is crucial to avoiding injury, so consult a coach, video, or book. If you don't own dumbbells, use milk jugs with handles, filled partly or fully with water.
Bicycling	Whether done on a stationary bike or outdoor bike, this is a non-weight-bearing exercise.	Check the comfort of the bike's seat. Ask if you can obtain a larger one, if desired.

Source: Adapted from information in U.S. Department of Health and Human Services, National Institutes of Health, "Active At Any Size!" http://www.win.niddk.nih.gov/publications/active.htm (accessed 9-19-06).

pain in joints, feet, ankles, or legs. Talk with your school nurse or health-care provider if you have any of these symptoms .

WEIGHT MANAGEMENT FOR YOUNG PEOPLE

When researchers compare the behaviors of overweight children and teens with the behaviors of normal-weight young people, they note some differences. In a study of adolescents in grades 7, 9, and 11, overweight girls and boys were more likely to skip breakfast, watch more television, and try out extreme diets than normal-weight adolescents. The overweight girls exercised fewer times a week and ate fewer servings of fruits and vegetables a day than the nonoverweight girls. The overweight boys in the survey reported eating more servings of high-fat and high-sugar snack foods than the nonoverweight boys.[1]

The behaviors of the overweight young people in this study contribute to an imbalance in energy intake versus energy output. Weight management for young people, though, is about more than listing harmful behaviors. More important is developing behaviors to promote nutritious eating, adequate physical activity, and overall well-being.

A committee of experts on obesity in young people developed the following recommendations for behavior goals, medical goals, and weight goals for overweight young people.[2]

Behavior Goals

Step 1. Do a mental survey of your eating habits and level of physical activity. Ask yourself how your family lifestyle influences the choices you make in these areas.

Step 2. Identify which behaviors are harmful to weight management and which are beneficial. For example, make lists of the high-calorie foods that you routinely overindulge in and the specific challenges to your being physically active.

Step 3. Make small, realistic changes in your behavior, a few at a time. Your goal is for these to become permanent lifestyle changes, so extreme or unrealistic goals are not an option. For example, reducing your energy intake by merely 100 calories per day can result in a weight loss of 10 pounds (4.5 kg) in a year.

Step 4. Monitor your progress with behavior changes, especially as your daily routine changes or when family habits change. Adjust your behaviors to deal with new challenges.

Medical Goals

Work with your family physician to track changes in your health, such as improvements in cholesterol levels, blood pressure, ability to be physically active, and emotional well-being.

Weight Goals

Your weight goals will depend on your age, your BMI-for-age, and whether you have health problems due to excess weight. Again, it is important to work with your physician to decide what is best for you.

If your BMI is between the 85th and 95th percentiles, you are considered at risk of overweight. If you have no health problems due to weight, your physician may advise weight maintenance, not weight loss. If you maintain a steady weight as you grow, your BMI-for-age gradually declines. But if you do have complications due to excess weight, your physician may recommend weight maintenance at first, followed by moderate weight loss. For instance, your first step may be to learn how to change behaviors so that you maintain your current weight for a while. Then, once these behaviors are in place, your next goal may be to shed about 1 pound (4.5 kg) per month.

A healthy goal for any overweight young person is to reach a BMI-for-age below the 85th percentile. More important than body mass index, however, are healthy eating and healthy levels of physical activity.

GOOD NEWS REGARDING WEIGHT MANAGEMENT

You may have heard that most overweight or obese people who lose a lot of weight eventually gain some or all of it back. However, it is important to remember that not everyone who loses weight regains it all. In one study participants lost an average of 66 pounds (30 kg) each and each person kept at least 30 pounds (14 kg) off for five years.[3] These people said they had increased self-confidence and an improved quality of life. Not only that, but they said that maintaining their new weight was easier than the process of losing the weight in the first place.

Young people who recognize and deal with their problems with excess weight give themselves a great advantage over people who wait until adulthood to address these matters. Researchers repeatedly point out that the longer a person carries extra poundage, the more likely he or she is to develop complications because of it. Conversely, the sooner a person reaches a healthy weight, or loses even 5 or 10 percent of their weight, the healthier that person can be.

As you carry out your plan to lose weight, become physically active, and modify behaviors that cause weight gain, don't be discouraged by occasional setbacks. Acknowledge

Five easy ways to be more physically active

1. While talking on the phone, walk around, do lunges or squats, or climb the stairs.

2. Instead of meeting friends for a movie, go dancing, walking, or hang out in a mall together.

3. Get to school early or stay late so you can walk once around the track.

4. While watching TV, do sit-ups or push-ups during commercial breaks.

5. Do volunteer work that requires movement, such as bathing dogs at a shelter, passing out books and magazines at a retirement home, or delivering groceries to shut-ins.

Five easy ways to cut calories

1. Eat off a smaller plate to make modest portions look plentiful.

2. Limit sugary drinks to one serving of juice a day. Drink water the rest of the time.

3. Eat sandwiches open-faced (no bread on top), or use a fork to eat the toppings off a pizza slice, skipping the crust.

4. Omit the cheese on a burger, leave three bites of burger uneaten, or leave ten french fries uneaten.

5. Take your own lunch to school instead of eating cafeteria food or vending machine snacks.

them as part of the process, then pick yourself up and get on with your plan. Find ways to reward yourself for sticking to your plan and taking small steps toward your goals. After all, you've earned it, one step at a time!

Myth: A crash diet is a good way to reach a healthy weight quickly.
Fact: Crash diets rarely result in permanent weight loss and are often deficient in nutrients.

7
DIETS, MEDICATIONS, AND SURGERY

As you have learned, a healthy plan for weight loss unfolds over a long period of time and involves lifestyle changes as well as basic changes in eating habits. Some people are able to make these changes on their own or with the support of friends or family. Others rely on guidance from a physician or nutritionist. Yet others realize that they may need more than just information and encouragement; that they should turn to a professionally structured weight-reduction program, medication, or even surgery.

STRUCTURED WEIGHT-REDUCTION PROGRAMS

There is no shortage of structured programs claiming to be your ticket to weight loss. They include commercialized diet plans that strictly limit your consumption of certain nutrients, calorie-reduction diets that focus on daily calorie counts, and support groups that combine diet advice with social support. Some of these programs are effective, while others, unfortunately, impose an imbalance in nutrient intake that can lead to health problems.

Commercialized Diet Plans

Commercialized diet plans spend big bucks on advertising to draw in hopeful customers. These are often flashy programs with books and celebrities providing media hype and success stories. Often these plans break away from the food pyramid guidelines by advocating that one or more nutrients or foods be consumed in unusually large or tiny proportions. For example, the Caveman Diet severely restricts carbohydrates while emphasizing protein and fats. Suzanne Somers's plan, Somersizing, bans many foods entirely, including potatoes, corn, white rice, most dairy products, nuts, sugar, flour, and bread.

Many commercialized diet plans are low-carbohydrate diets. Advocates claim that keeping the body's production of insulin low (by limiting carbohydrates) prevents storage of excess body fat and reduces existing fat reserves. Typically, low-carb diets restrict or prohibit foods such as breads, grains, certain fruits and vegetables, and sweets. Most of the low-carb diet is made up of protein-rich foods such as meat, fish, poultry, and dairy products. Dieters may be encouraged to eat unlimited amounts of carbohydrate-free foods. Examples of low-carbohydrate diets include the Atkins Diet, the South Beach Diet, the Zone Diet, and Sugar Busters.

Following a low-carb diet usually does lead to weight loss. However, there are drawbacks. Much of the initial weight loss is water loss due to low glycogen reserves in the body. Also, the small choice of foods limits the range of nutrients ingested. Water loss and nutrient loss can lead to dehydration, low potassium, and ketosis. The high levels of saturated fat being consumed can lead to heart disease. Many such dieters lose weight simply because of their boredom with the limited food choices. When they return to a balanced diet or gradually admit carbs into their diet, they regain weight.

Calorie-Reduction Diets

Some diet plans focus on reducing calories rather than restricting a particular type of food. Calorie-reduction diets include food-exchange plans, preportioned food plans, liquid meal plans, and very-low-calorie diets (VLCDs). One advantage to these programs is that most of them focus on a balanced intake of nutrients, which promotes success since dieters are not required to give up favorite foods.

Food-exchange programs use groups of food to create meal plans. The foods within each group have about the same number of calories and amount of nutrients. The dieter selects a certain number of servings from each group to make up meals and snacks. These programs are usually nutritionally balanced, and they appeal to diverse appetites. As well, they teach food selection techniques that are usable in the long run, both at home and when eating out.

The American Diabetes Association and the American Dietetic Association have published meal planning exchange lists. These lists are used by dieticians and diabetes educators. Some independently created diet plans use these exchange lists, too.

Preportioned food plans provide you with prepackaged meals that are nutritionally balanced and have a controlled number of calories. You combine the packaged meals to meet each day's needs for nutrients and calories. Everything is taken care of, from portion sizes to nutrition to calorie counts. Relying on prepackaged meals is a convenient way to create a nutritious, low-calorie diet. The meals can be expensive, however. Another drawback is that this type of program makes a dieter dependent on the program rather than teaching him or her how to plan meals and snacks on his or her own. Examples of this type of diet include Jenny Craig and Nutrisystem.

Liquid-meal plans are a lot like preportioned meal plans

except that nutrients are provided in a drinkable format. Typically, you are advised to replace one or two meals a day with liquid meals and to eat a nutritionally balanced meal of regular foods for the remaining meal(s) and for planned snacks. As with preportioned meals, liquid meals make it easy for you to count and control the intake of calories. Nonetheless, relying on liquid meals in the long run can be inconvenient, boring, and unrealistic. Typically, these programs have high drop-out rates. Perhaps the best known liquid-meal program is Slim-Fast. It is worth noting that many health-care providers consider liquid-meal plans to be a form of very-low-calorie diet.

Very-low-calorie diets (VLCDs) restrict caloric intake to fewer than 800 calories a day. These diets include a relatively large amount of protein with small amounts of carbohydrates and fats. They may take the form of liquid meals or may use regular foods. VLCDs are supplemented to provide sufficient vitamins, minerals, and electrolytes. Since this diet cuts calories so severely, it is appropriate only for people who are at least 30 to 40 percent overweight. Also, VLCDs are not recommended for people over age 50 or those with certain health problems, such as type 1 diabetes, or who have suffered a recent heart attack.

Even though current-day VLCDs are safe when administered properly by a physician, they are not a magic cure. On the plus side, they can result in the loss of over a pound and a half (.68 kg) a day during the first week, dropping to just over half a pound (.23 kg) a day by the third week. This weight decrease can promote reduced blood cholesterol levels, lowered blood pressure, improved breathing, and improved glucose tolerance. On the downside, most of the early weight drop is due to water loss. The patient must stick faithfully to the plan to lose body fat. High dropout rates are common, and most people who complete the program regain the weight later. Side effects of VLCDs include fatigue, light-headedness, nervousness, constipation, diarrhea, dry skin, thinning hair, anemia, and menstrual irregularities. The FDA requires all VLCD programs to carry the warning that they can lead to serious illness and also must be administered under proper medical supervision.

Diet Support Groups

Diet support groups assist and encourage people as they lose weight and learn to maintain a goal weight. They help members create nutritious meal plans together with safe programs of physical activity. Meetings may include weigh-ins, informative talks, and inspirational conversation. The emphasis is on slow, steady, maintainable weight loss and, ultimately, on weight maintenance. Programs such as Weight Watchers and TOPS Club, Inc. (Take Off Pounds Sensibly) charge fees, though amounts vary. What one program charges for a couple of weeks may be the same as what another program charges for a year. Some programs, such as Overeaters Anonymous, do not charge a fee, although contributions are accepted.

MEDICATIONS FOR WEIGHT LOSS

Medications for weight loss make you feel full after eating only a little food. They can prevent your body from absorbing up to a third of the fat you eat. Sounds great, doesn't it? The truth is, weight-loss medications are not the best choice for most people who are overweight or obese. Typically, these drugs are prescribed only to people who have health problems requiring immediate weight reduction or who have tried modifying their diet and behaviors with discouraging results. And even those patients with the medication are required to reduce their calorie intake and increase their physical activity.

Prescription medication, combined with reduced-calorie meal plans and adequate physical activity, can result in a drop of 5 to 10 percent of body weight in a year. Most of the weight goes during the first six months. Studies disclose that many people gain back some of the weight during the second year. When dieters stop taking the weight-loss drug, they almost always regain all the weight they lost. Consequently, someone wishing to use medication as a means of getting thinner would have to take the drug indefinitely to keep off even some of the lost weight. Another major drawback is that, since the weight-loss drugs in use today are relatively new, long-term effects are unknown.

Many weight-loss aids are sold over the counter (OTC) as opposed to being sold by prescription only. OTC diet drugs are available in pill, capsule, gel, powder, and liquid forms. These drugs typically contain a long list of ingredients that may include herbs, plants (called botanicals), vitamins, minerals, caffeine, and laxatives, to name a few possibilities. Unlike prescription diet drugs, OTC diet drugs are not regulated by the U.S. Food and Drug Administration (FDA). Consequently, consumers wonder, with good reason, how to tell whether the weight-loss aids they see on drugstore shelves or on the Internet are effective and whether they are safe.

DANGEROUS DIET DRUGS

Most nonprescription weight-loss aids have not been proven safe or effective. The long-term effects of most of them are not yet known. Some products or ingredients, such as ephedra, have been proven dangerous and have been pulled from the market by the FDA. To learn more about specific herbal or dietary supplements, read the chart on pages 84 and 85, prepared by the Mayo Clinic.

In 1996 American doctors wrote 18 million prescriptions

for a diet drug called fen-phen.[1] The drug was a combination of the appetite suppressants fenfluramine and phentermine. For years, the popularity of fen-phen had been growing, and many people attributed their weight loss successes to taking the drug.

In 1997 news broke that some fen-phen users were having heart valve problems. One study of twenty-four women showed that even though none of them had a previous history of heart disease, they all developed heart valve trouble while taking the drug.[2] The FDA found that up to 30 percent of fen-phen users could have heart valve abnormalities, even if they had no symptoms.[3] Fen-phen was pulled from the market. Fenfluramine was identified as the source of the health problems. The other appetite suppressant in the medication, phentermine, continues to be prescribed.

Another diet aid that has been linked to health problems is ephedra, an herbal extract. Used in dietary supplements, ephedra was touted as an aid to weight loss and increased athletic performance. In the early 2000s, however, investigations into reports of ephedra-related health problems uncovered claims of two deaths, three heart attacks, nine strokes, three seizures, and five psychiatric cases.[4] Ephedra is now banned for sale in the United States by the FDA.

SURGERY FOR WEIGHT LOSS

Doctors evaluate candidates for weight-loss surgery very carefully. Typically, patients have a body mass index above 40 and/or weight-related health problems that make the surgery worth the risks. Doctors also take into account candidates' past efforts to lose weight, their willingness to make lifestyle changes, and their understanding of the risks involved. Patients are counseled and monitored by health-care professionals, both before and after the surgery.

Herbal or dietary supplement	The claims	What you need to know
Bitter orange	Decreases appetite	• Touted as an "ephedra substitute," but may cause problems similar to those of ephedra • Long-term effects unknown
Chitosan	Blocks the absorption of dietary fat	• Relatively safe, but unlikely to cause weight loss • Can cause constipation, bloating, and other gastrointestinal complaints • Long-term effects unknown
Chromium	Reduces body fat and builds muscle	• Relatively safe, but unlikely to cause weight loss • Long-term effects unknown
Conjugated linoleic acid (CLA)	Reduces body fat, decreases appetite, and builds muscle	• Might decrease body fat and increase muscle, but isn't likely to reduce total body weight • Can cause diarrhea, indigestion, and other gastrointestinal problems
Country mallow (heartleaf)	Decreases appetite and increases the number of calories burned	• Contains ephedra, which is dangerous • Likely unsafe and should be avoided

Herbal or dietary supplement	The claims	What you need to know
Ephedra	Decreases appetite	• Can cause high blood pressure, heart rate irregularities, sleeplessness, seizures, heart attacks, strokes, and even death • Banned from the marketplace because of safety concerns, but may still be legally sold as a tea • Despite the ban, many ephedra products still sold on the Internet
Green tea extract	Increases calorie and fat metabolism and decreases appetite	• Limited evidence to support the claim • Can cause vomiting, bloating, indigestion, and diarrhea • May contain a large amount of caffeine
Guar gum	Blocks the absorption of dietary fat and increases the feeling of fullness, which leads to decreased calorie intake	• Relatively safe, but unlikely to cause weight loss • Can cause diarrhea, flatulence, and other gastrointestinal problems
Hoodia	Decreases appetite	• No conclusive evidence to support the claim

Source: Mayo Clinic Staff, "Weight-loss pills: What can diet aids do for you?" http://www.mayoclinic.com/health/weight-loss/HQ01160 (accessed 9-22-06.)

After the surgery, weight loss takes place over the next eighteen to twenty-four months. Some weight may be regained following the initial weight reduction. For patients who are committed to making permanent changes in eating and exercise habits, surgery can lead to a lower body weight that is maintained in the long run. In one study, patients were weighed three years after their surgery. About three-fourths of them showed a loss of half the excess weight from before the surgery.[5] While these weight-loss numbers may vary from study to study, the good news is that most patients who have had weight-loss surgery do maintain a healthier weight in the long run.

There are two main types of weight-loss surgery, also called bariatric surgery. A restrictive surgery makes the stomach smaller, restricting the amount of food the patient can eat at one time. A malabsorptive surgery decreases the absorption of calories in the small intestine. A malabsorptive surgery is typically performed in conjunction with a restrictive surgery rather than alone.

One type of restrictive surgery is vertical-banded gastroplasty, sometimes called stomach stapling. Using staples, the surgeon creates a small, tube-like pouch in the top of the stomach. The surgeon uses a plastic band to cinch the lower end of the pouch, leaving a tiny opening for food to pass through to the larger

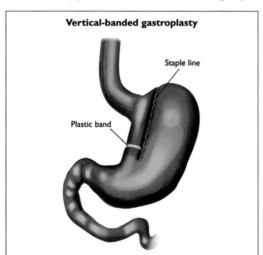

Vertical-banded gastroplasty

Staple line

Plastic band

Stomach stapling surgery makes the size of the usable stomach smaller.

part of the stomach. Since patients can eat only a half cup to a cup of food before feeling uncomfortably full, they consume fewer calories. In turn, the reduced calorie intake promotes weight loss.

The small opening from the pouch into the rest of the stomach prevents bulky foods, like meats and grains, from passing quickly into the stomach. One drawback is that soft foods, such as ice cream, soft drinks, and other high-calorie treats, can pass easily through the banded opening.

Gastric banding, also a restrictive surgery, is newer than vertical-banded gastroplasty. It uses an adjustable band to partition off a pouch in the top part of the stomach, leaving a tiny opening to the rest of the stomach. A health-care professional can adjust the size of the opening by inflating or deflating the band. (For this reason, the surgery is sometimes called *adjustable* gastric banding.) The small pouch holds only an ounce or two of food, so patients can eat very little in a sitting.

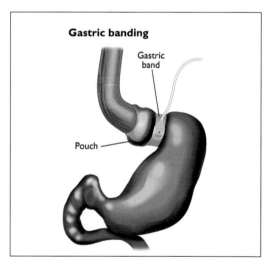

After gastric banding, an adjustable band controls the size of the opening to the stomach.

As a result, they consume fewer calories. As with vertical-banded gastroplasty, consuming fewer calories helps patients lose weight. Gastric banding surgery was approved by the FDA in 2001.

A gastric bypass involves both a restrictive surgery and a

malabsorptive surgery. The most common gastric bypass is the Roux-en-Y gastric bypass. The surgeon makes the stomach smaller by using, for example, staples or a plastic band. He or she connects this small pouch to the middle part of the small intestine (jejunum). As a result, food bypasses the larger part of the stomach and the upper part of the small intestine (duodenum).

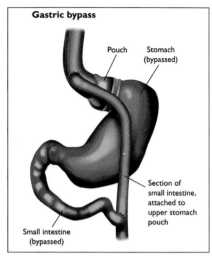

Gastric bypass

Pouch

Stomach (bypassed)

Section of small intestine, attached to upper stomach pouch

Small intestine (bypassed)

A gastric bypass routes food from a tiny pouch in the stomach to the jejunum.

As with the other weight-loss surgeries discussed here, the smaller stomach resulting from a gastric bypass helps patients feel full with only a small amount of food. In addition, since food passes from the small stomach to the jejunum, bypassing the duodenum, fewer calories are absorbed.

Weight-loss surgeries carry risks, as do all surgeries. A primary risk is an infection at the incision. Another risk is a leak from the stomach into the abdominal cavity, resulting in an infection called peritonitis. One-third or more of patients develop gallstones.

Weight-loss surgery patients are also at risk for nutritional deficiencies such as anemia or osteoporosis. Ideally, they work with a dietician to plan menus to address their unique nutritional needs. For the rest of their lives, they need vitamin and mineral supplements.

Some patients need follow-up surgeries to correct complications of their weight-loss surgery. Complications may include pulled staples, band slippage, and abdominal hernias.

The plastic band may begin to wear through the wall of the stomach. The connection between the stomach and the intestines may constrict, leading to nausea and vomiting after eating. The bypassed stomach may enlarge, resulting in hiccups and bloating.

People who have had a malabsorptive surgery may experience dumping syndrome. This is caused by food moving too quickly through the stomach and intestines. Just after eating, the person may feel nauseated, faint, sweaty, or extremely weak. He or she may have to lie down until the symptoms pass. Occasionally, diarrhea occurs after meals.

The risk of death from weight-loss surgery is slight. Fewer than 3 in 200 people die after weight-loss surgery.

No matter what kind of weight-loss assistance you choose, remember that your long-term success depends on reducing caloric intake, getting enough physical exercise, and making the commitment to lifestyle changes. No diet plan, pill, or surgery can replace these principles. Rather, these options are intended to work together with the basic principles to help you reach success in especially challenging circumstances. Further, it is crucial that young people wishing to lose weight consult a professional who can help them to choose the best weight-loss solution for their age and stage of physical development.

APPENDIXES

Appendix A

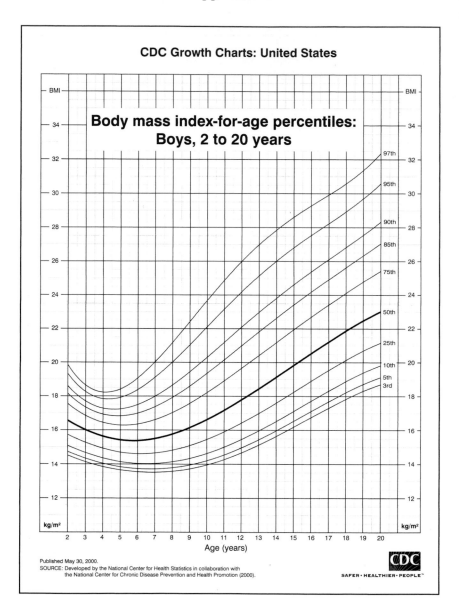

A BMI-for-age less than the 5th percentile indicates underweight. A BMI between the 5th and 84th percentiles indicates a normal weight. A BMI between the 85th and 94th percentiles indicates a risk of overweight, and a BMI greater than or equal to the 95th percentile indicates overweight.

Appendix B

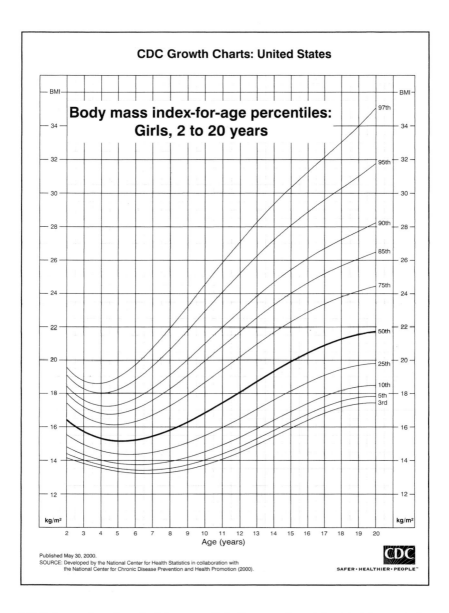

A BMI-for-age less than the 5th percentile indicates underweight. A BMI between the 5th and 84th percentiles indicates a normal weight. A BMI between the 85th and 94th percentiles indicates a risk of overweight, and a BMI greater than or equal to the 95th percentile indicates overweight .

Appendix C

Dietary Reference Intakes (DRIs): Recommended Intakes for Individuals, Total Water and Macronutrients
Food and Nutrition Board, Institute of Medicine, National Academies

Life Stage Group	Total Water[a] (L/d)	Carbo-hydrate (g/d)	Total Fiber (g/d)	Fat (g/d)	Linoleic Acid (g/d)	a-Linolenic Acid (g/d)	Protein (g/d)
Infants							
0-6 mo	0.7*	60*	ND	31*	4.4*	0.5*	9.1*
7-12 mo	0.8*	95*	ND	30*	4.6*	0.5*	**11.0+**
Children							
1-3 y	1.3*	**130**	19*	ND	7*	0.7*	**13**
4-8 y	1.7*	**130**	25*	ND	10*	0.9*	**19**
Males							
9-13 y	2.4*	**130**	31*	ND	12*	1.2*	**34**
14-18 y	3.3*	**130**	38*	ND	16*	1.6*	**52**
19-30 y	3.7*	**130**	38*	ND	17*	1.6*	**56**
31-50 y	3.7*	**130**	38*	ND	17*	1.6*	**56**
51-70 y	3.7*	**130**	30*	ND	14*	1.6*	**56**
>70 y	3.7*	**130**	30*	ND	14*	1.6*	**56**
Females							
9-13 y	2.1*	**130**	26*	ND	10*	1.0*	**34**
14-18 y	2.3*	**130**	26*	ND	11*	1.1*	**46**
19-30 y	2.7*	**130**	25*	ND	12*	1.1*	**46**
31-50 y	2.7*	**130**	25*	ND	12*	1.1*	**46**
51-70 y	2.7*	**130**	21*	ND	11*	1.1*	**46**
>70 y	2.7*	**130**	21*	ND	11*	1.1*	**46**
Pregnancy							
14-18 y	3.0*	**175**	28*	ND	13*	1.4*	**71**
19-30 y	3.0*	**175**	28*	ND	13*	1.4*	**71**
31-50 y	3.0*	**175**	28*	ND	13*	1.4*	**71**
Lactation							
14-18 y	3.8*	**210**	29*	ND	13*	1.3*	**71**
19-30 y	3.8*	**210**	29*	ND	13*	1.3*	**71**
31-50 y	3.8*	**210**	29*	ND	13*	1.3*	**71**

NOTE: This table represents Recommended Dietary Allowances (RDAs) in bold type and Adequate Intakes (AIs) in ordinary type followed by an asterisk (*). RDAs and AIs may both be used as goals for individual intake. RDAs are set to meet the needs of almost all (97 to 98 percent) individuals in a group. For healthy breastfed infants, the AI is the mean intake. The AI for other life stage and gender groups is believed to cover the needs of all individuals in the group, but lack of data or uncertainty in the data prevent being able to specify with confidence the percentage of individuals covered by this intake. The plus (+) symbol indicates a change from the prepublication copy due to a calculation error.
a Total water includes all water contained in food, beverages, and drinking water.
b Based on g protein per kg of body weight for the reference body weight, e.g., for adults 0.8 /kg body weight for the reference body weight.
c Not determined.
SOURCES: *Dietary Reference Intakes for Energy, Carbohydrate, Fiber, Fat, Fatty Acids, Cholesterol, Protein, and Amino Acids (2002/2005); Dietary Reference Intakes for Water, Potassium, Sodium, Chloride, and Sulfate (2005).* These reports may be accessed via http://www.nap.edu.

Appendix D

Reference Intakes (DRIs): Acceptable Macronutrient Distribution Ranges
Food and Nutrition Board, Institute of Medicine, National Academies

	Range (percent of energy)		
Macronutrient	Children, 1-3 y	Children, 4-18 y	Adults
Fat	30-40	25-35	20-35
n-6 Polyunsaturated fatty acids[a] (linoleic acid)	5-10	5-10	5-10
n-3 Polyunsaturated fatty acids[a] (a-linolenic acid)	0.6-1.2	0.6-1.2	0.6-1.2
Carbohydrate	45-65	45-65	45-65
Protein	5-20	10-30	10-35

a Approximately 10 percent of the total can come from loner-chain n-3 or n-6 fatty acids.

SOURCE: *Dietary Reference Intakes for Energy, Carbohydrate, Fiber, Fat, Fatty Acids, Cholesterol, Protein, and Amino Acids* (2002/2005).

Appendix E

Dietary Reference Intakes: Recommended Intakes for Individuals: Vitamins

Life Stage Group	Vitamin A (µg/day)[a]	Vitamin C (mg/day)	Vitamin D (µg/day)[b,c]	Vitamin E (mg/day)[d]	Vitamin K (µg/day)	Thiamin (mg/day)	Riboflavin (mg/day)	Niacin (mg/day)[e]	Vitamin B$_6$ (mg/day)	Folate (µg/day)[f]	Vitamin B$_{12}$ (µg/day)	Pantothenic Acid (mg/day)	Biotin (µg/day)	Choline (mg/day)
Infants														
0-6 mo	400*	40*	5*	4*	2.0*	0.2*	0.3*	2*	0.1*	65*	0.4*	1.7*	5*	125*
7-12 mo	500*	50*	5*	5*	2.5*	0.3*	0.4*	4*	0.3*	80*	0.5*	1.8*	6*	150*
Children														
1-3 y	300	15	5*	6	30*	0.5	0.5	6	0.5	150	0.9	2*	8*	200*
4-8 y	400	25	5*	7	55*	0.6	0.6	8	0.5	200	1.2	3*	12*	250*
Males														
9-13 y	600	45	5*	11	60*	0.9	0.9	12	1.0	300	1.8	4*	20*	315*
14-18 y	900	75	5*	15	75*	1.2	1.3	16	1.3	400	2.4	5*	25*	550*
19-30 y	900	90	5*	15	120*	1.2	1.3	16	1.3	400	2.4	5*	30*	550*
31-50 y	900	90	5*	15	120*	1.2	1.3	16	1.3	400	2.4	5*	30*	550*
51-70 y	900	90	10*	15	120*	1.2	1.3	16	1.7	400	2.4[h]	5*	30*	550*
>70 y	900	90	15*	15	120*	1.2	1.3	16	1.7	400	2.4[h]	5*	30*	550*
Females														
9-13 y	600	45	5*	11	60*	0.9	0.9	12	1.0	300	1.8	4*	20*	375*
14-18 y	700	65	5*	15	75*	1.0	1.0	14	1.2	400[i]	2.4	5*	25*	400*
19-30 y	700	75	5*	15	90*	1.1	1.1	14	1.3	400[i]	2.4	5*	30*	425*
31-50 y	700	75	5*	15	90*	1.1	1.1	14	1.3	400[i]	2.4	5*	30*	425*
51-70 y	700	75	10*	15	90*	1.1	1.1	14	1.5	400	2.4[h]	5*	30*	425*
>70 y	700	75	15*	15	90*	1.1	1.1	14	1.5	400	2.4[h]	5*	30*	425*
Pregnancy														
≤18 y	750	80	5*	15	75*	1.4	1.4	18	1.9	600[j]	2.6	6*	30*	450*
14-18 y	770	85	5*	15	90*	1.4	1.4	18	1.9	600[j]	2.6	6*	30*	450*
19-30 y	770	85	5*	15	90*	1.4	1.4	18	1.9	600[j]	2.6	6*	30*	450*
Lactation														
≤18 y	1200	115	5*	19	75*	1.4	1.6	17	2.0	500	2.8	7*	35*	550*
14-18 y	1300	120	5*	19	90*	1.4	1.6	17	2.0	500	2.8	7*	35*	550*
19-30 y	1300	120	5*	19	90*	1.4	1.6	17	2.0	500	2.8	7*	35*	550*

NOTE: This table (taken from the DRI reports, see www.nap.edu) presents Recommended Dietary Allowances (RDAs) in **bold** type and Adequate Intakes (AIs) in ordinary type followed by an asterisk (*). RDAs and AIs may both be used as goals for individual intakes. RDAs are set up to meet the needs of almost all (97–98%) individuals in a group. For healthy breastfed infants, the AI is the mean intake. The AI for all other life stage and gender groups is believed to cover needs of all individuals in the group, but lack of data or uncertainty in the data prevent being able to specify with confidence the percentage of individuals covered by this intake.

[a] As retinol activity equivalents (RAEs). 1 RAE = 1 µg retinol, 12 µg β-carotene, 24 µg β-carotene, or 24 µg β-cryptoxanthin in foods. To calculate RAEs from REs of provitamin A carotenoids in foods, divide RE by 2. For preformed vitamin A in foods or supplements and for provitamin A carotenoids in supplements, 1 RE = 1 RAE.

[b] Cholecalciferol. 1 µg cholecalciferol = 40 IU vitamin D.

[c] In the absence of exposure to adequate sunlight.

[d] As α-tocopherol, which includes RRR-α-tocopherol, the only form of α-tocopherol that occurs naturally in foods, and the 2R-stereoisomeric forms of α-tocopherol (RRR-, RSR-, RRS-, and RSS-α-tocopherol). Does not include the 2S-stereoisomeric forms of α-tocopherol (SRR-, SSR-, SRS-, and SSS- α -tocopherol), also found in food and supplements.

[e] As niacin equivalents (NEs), 1mg niacin = 60 mg tryptophan; 0-6 months = preformed niacin (not NE).

[f] As dietary folate equivalents (DFEs. 1 DFE = 1 µg food folate = 0.6 µg folic acid from fortified food or as a supplement consumed with food = 0.5 µg of a supplement taken on an empty stomach.

[g] Although AIs have been set for choline, there are few data to assess whether a dietary supplement of choline is needed at all stages of the life cycle, and it may be that the choline requirement can be met by endogenous synthesis at some of these stages.

[h] Because 10-30% of older people may malabsorb food-bound B$_{12}$, it is advisable for those older than 50 years to meet their RFD mainly by consuming foods fortified with B$_{12}$ or containing B$_{12}$.

[i] In view of evidence linking folate intake with neural tube defects in the fetus, it is recommended that all women capable of becoming pregnant consume 400 µg from supplements or fortified foods in addition to intake of food folate from a varied diet.

[j] It is assumed that women will consume 400 µg from supplements or fortified foods until their pregnancy is confirmed and they enter prenatal care, which ordinarily occurs after the end of the periconceptional period – the critical time for neural tube formation.

Appendix F

Dietary Reference Intakes: Recommended Intakes for Individuals: Minerals

Life Stage Group	Calcium (mg/day)	Chromium (µg/day)	Copper (µg/day)	Fluoride (mg/day)	Iodine (µg/day)	Iron (mg/day)	Magnesium (mg/day)	Manganese (mg/day)	Molybdenum (µg/day)	Phosphorus (mg/day)	Selenium (µg/day)	Zinc (mg/day)
Infants												
0-6 mo	210*	0.2*	200*	0.01*	110*	0.27*	30*	0.003*	2*	100*	15*	2*
7-12 mo	270*	5.5*	220*	0.5*	130*	11	75*	0.6*	3*	275*	20*	3
Children												
1-3 y	500*	11*	340	0.7*	90	7	80	1.2*	17	460	20	3
4-8 y	800*	15*	440	1*	90	10	130	1.5*	22	500	30	5
Males												
9-13 y	1,300*	25*	700	2*	120	8	240	1.9*	34	1,250	40	8
14-18 y	1,300*	35*	890	3*	150	11	410	2.2*	43	1,250	55	11
19-30 y	1,000*	35*	900	4*	150	8	400	2.3*	45	700	55	11
31-50 y	1,000*	35*	900	4*	150	8	420	2.3*	45	700	55	11
51-70 y	1,200*	30*	900	4*	150	8	420	2.3*	45	700	55	11
>70 y	1,200*	30*	900	4*	150	8	420	2.3*	45	700	55	11
Females												
9-13 y	1,300*	21*	700	2*	120	8	240	1.6*	34	1,250	40	8
14-18 y	1,300*	24*	890	3*	150	15	360	1.6*	43	1,250	55	9
19-30 y	1,000*	25*	900	3*	150	18	310	1.8*	45	700	55	8
31-50 y	1,000*	25*	900	3*	150	18	320	1.8*	45	700	55	8
51-70 y	1,200*	20*	900	3*	150	8	320	1.8*	45	700	55	8
>70 y	1,200*	20*	900	3*	150	8	320	1.8*	45	700	55	8
Pregnancy												
≤18 y	1,300*	29*	1,000	3*	220	27	400	2.0*	50	1,250	60	13
14-18 y	1,000*	30*	1,000	3*	220	27	350	2.0*	50	700	60	11
19-30 y	1,000*	30*	1,000	3*	220	27	360	2.0*	50	700	60	11
Lactation												
≤18 y	1,300*	44*	1,300	3*	290	10	360	2.6*	50	1,250	60	14
14-18 y	1,300*	45*	1,300	3*	290	9	310	2.6*	50	700	60	12
19-30 y	1,300*	45*	1,300	3*	290	9	320	2.6*	50	700	60	12

NOTE: This table (taken from the DRI reports, see www.nap.edu) presents Recommended Dietary Allowances (RDAs) in **bold** type and Adequate Intakes (AIs) in ordinary type followed by an asterisk (*). RDAs and AIs may both be used as goals for individual intakes. RDAs are set up to meet the needs of almost all (97-98%) individuals in a group. For healthy breastfed infants, the AI is the mean intake. The AI for all other life stage and gender groups is believed to cover needs of all individuals in the group, but lack of data or uncertainty in the data prevents being able to specify with confidence the percentage of individuals covered by this intake.

Metric Conversion Chart

You can use the chart below to convert from U.S. measurements to the metric system.

Weight
1 ounce = 28 grams
1/2 pound (8) ounces = 227 grams

1 pound = .45 kilogram
2.2 pounds = 1 kilogram

Liquid Volume
1 teaspoon = 5 milliliters
1 tablespoon = 15 milliliters
1 fluid ounce = 30 milliliters
1 cup = 240 milliliters
1 pint = 480 milliliters
1 quart = .95 liter

Length
1/4 inch = .6 centimeter
1/2 inch = 1.25 centimeters

1 inch = 2.5 centimeters

Temperature
100°F = 40°C
110°F = 45°C
350°F = 180°C
375°F = 190°C
400°F = 200°C
425°F = 220°C
450°F = 235°C

Body Mass Index Conversion Formula (Metric)

$$BMI = \left(\frac{\text{weight in kilograms}}{(\text{height in meters}) \times (\text{height in meters})} \right) \times 703$$

NOTES

Chapter 1

1. Lowry, Richard et al., p. 323.

2. Lowry et al., p. 320. Paxton, Valois, and Drane, p. 136.

3. Lowry et al., p. 320.

4. National Center for Health Statistics, "Prevalence of Overweight and Obesity Among Adults: United States, 1999—2002." Figure 2.

5. Ibid., Figure 1, "Prevalence of Overweight Among Children and Adoloescents: United States, 1999—2002," Figure 1.

6. National Center for Health Statistics, "Obesity Still a Major Problem, New Data Show."

7. Centers for Disease Control and Prevention (CDC). "Overweight and Obesity: Obesity Trends: U.S. Obesity Trends 1985—2005."

8. Adapted from the United States Department of Health and Human Services, "The Surgeon General's Call to Action to Prevent and Decrease Overweight and Obesity."

9. Hensrud, Donald D., ed., *Mayo Clinic on Healthy Weight*, p. 8.

10. United States Department of Health and Human Services, "The Surgeon General's Call to Action to Prevent and Decrease Overweight and Obesity."

11. Brownell, Kelly D., "The Environment and Obesity," p. 434.

12. Centers for Disease Control and Prevention, "Overweight and Obesity: Contributing Factors."

Chapter 2

1. Boutelle, et al. p. 532.

2. Lowry, Richard, et al., p. 320. Paxton, Valois, and Drane, p. 136.

3. United States Department of Health and Human Services, "Choosing a Safe and Successful Weight-loss Program."

Chapter 3

1. Manson, Skerrett, and Willett, p. 424.

2. American Heart Association, "High Blood Pressure, Factors That Contribute To."

3. World Health Organization.

4. Needham and Crosnoe, p. 49.

5. Lawson, "The Obesity-Depression Link."

6. United States Department of Health and Human Services, "Overweight and Obesity: At a Glance: The Facts About Overweight and Obesity."

7. Latner and Strunkard, "Getting Worse: The Stigmatization of Obese Children."

8. Yanovski, Susan Z., p. 404.

9. Tamborlane, William V., ed., p. 129. Grilo, Carlos M., p. 180.

10. Mellin, Alison E. et al., p. 148.

11. Centers for Disease Control and Prevention, "Overweight and Obesity: Frequently Asked Questions."

Chapter 4

1. Tamborlane, ed., p. 240.

Chapter 6

1. Mellin, p. 148.

2. Barlow, Sarah E., and William H. Dietz, p. 6.

3. Hensrud, ed., *Mayo Clinic: Healthy Weight for Everybody*, p. 119.

Chapter 7

1. Hensrud, *Mayo Clinic on Healthy Weight*, p. 177.

2. Ibid.

3. Ibid.

4. Smolin and Grosvenor, p. 110.

5. Hensrud, *Mayo Clinic on Healthy Weight*, p. 185.

GLOSSARY

active lifestyle: Having a daily routine involving exertion that raises the body's temperature.

antioxidant: A substance such as vitamin E, vitamin C, or beta carotene that is believed to protect body cells from the damaging effects of oxygen in tissues.

binge eating disorder: An eating disorder characterized by recurring episodes of eating huge amounts of food. People with this disorder do not engage in purging behaviors.

body image: How you feel "in your own skin," how you think others see you, and how you think you measure up to physical standards set by yourself and others.

body mass index (BMI): A measurement of body fat in relation to body height. The regular body mass index is intended for adults. BMI-for-age is the calculation used for children and adolescents.

calorie: The amount of heat energy required to raise the temperature of 1 gram of water by 1 degree Celsius at 1 atmospheric pressure. The energy in food is measured in calories.

carbohydrates: Sugars, starches, and most fibers: one of the six classes of nutrients. *Simple carbohydrates* are naturally occurring sugars, such as fructose in fruit; they are a source of quick energy. *Complex carbohydrates* provide longer-lasting energy and are found in most grain products, vegetables, and potatoes.

cooldown: The part of an exercise activity that helps your body return to a normal temperature and rate of breathing.

diet: A pattern of eating; often used to refer to a weight-loss plan of eating.

dietary reference intakes (DRIs): Recommended daily amounts of nutrients.

digestive process: The body's way of breaking down food so that nutrients and energy can be absorbed.

eating disorder: A pattern of eating intended to control weight that is actually destructive to the person's physical and psychological health.

food-exchange program: A weight-loss or weight-management system that uses "food exchanges," or groups of food, to create meal plans.

gastric banding: A weight-loss surgery that uses an adjustable band to make a small pouch at the top part of the stomach with a tiny opening to the rest of the stomach.

gastric bypass: A weight-loss surgery that makes the stomach smaller by using, for example, staples or a plastic band, and routes food from this smaller stomach to the middle part of the small intestine.

glycogen: A polysaccharide, molecularly similar to starch, that is the main form of carbohydrate storage in animals. It occurs mainly in liver and muscle tissue. It is readily converted to glucose to be used as energy by the body.

hypertension: High blood pressure.

lipids: Fats: one of the six classes of nutrients.

liquid-meal plan: A weight-loss method that provides nutrients in drinkable meals.

low-carbohydrate diet: A weight-loss method that limits consumption of high-carbohydrate foods on the premise that carbohydrates raise the body's production of insulin and, in turn, the increased insulin promotes the storage of body fat and can trigger hunger.

malabsorptive surgery: A weight-loss surgery that causes a decrease in the absorption of calories in the small intestine.

metabolism: All of the chemical processes in your body that together keep your cells healthy and keep you alive.

minerals: Inorganic substances: one of the six classes of nutrients.

moderately active lifestyle: Having a daily routine involving standing and walking.

non-weight-bearing activity: An activity that puts little or no extra stress on your joints.

nutrients: Substances needed by the body for energy and tissue-building. The six classes of nutrients are carbohydrates, protein, lipids, vitamins, minerals, and water.

nutrition: The means by which a living organism takes in and uses nourishment for energy, growth, and repair. Also the science that studies the processes of organisms and food.

obese: Having a body mass index (BMI) greater than 30 as an adult.

preportioned food plan: A weight-loss or weight-management system consisting of prepackaged meals that are nutritionally balanced and have set numbers of calories.

protein: Chains of amino acids: one of the six classes of nutrients. It is found in animal products such as eggs and meat, and certain vegetables, grains, and beans.

resting metabolic rate (RMR): The amount of energy your body expends when awake but resting, not digesting food, and neither hot nor cold.

restrictive surgery: A weight-loss surgery that makes the stomach smaller, restricting the amount of food the patient can eat at one time.

satiety: A feeling of fullness or satisfaction after eating.

sedentary lifestyle: Having a daily routine that involves mostly sitting.

self-image: How you see yourself; how you assess your personal qualities and individual worth. Self-image incorporates your body image.

stroke: A sudden loss of brain function caused by the rupture or blockage of a blood vessel in the brain.

triglycerides: Fats in the diet, including saturated fats and unsaturated fats.

type 2 diabetes: A disease characterized by raised levels of glucose in the blood due to the body's inability to use insulin properly.

vertical-banded gastroplasty: A weight-loss surgery that uses staples to make a small pouch in the top of the stomach and a plastic band to cinch the lower end of the pouch, leaving a tiny opening to the rest of the stomach.

very-low-calorie diet (VLCD): A weight-loss method that restricts calorie intake to fewer than 800 calories a day. It includes a relatively large amount of protein and small amounts of carbohydrates and fats, and may be administrated as liquid meals or regular foods.

vitamins: Organic substances found in tiny amounts in plant and animal foods: one of the six classes of nutrients.

warm-up: The part of an exercise activity that prepares your body for the more vigorous movements to follow.

water: An odorless, tasteless liquid: one of the six classes of nutrients. An adult's body is made up of 60 to 70 percent water.

weight-bearing activity: An activity involving lifting weights or using your own body as a weight.

wellness: A state of physical and mental good health.

FURTHER INFORMATION

Books

Bauchner, Elizabeth. *What Do I Have to Lose?: A Teen's Guide to Weight Management.* Philadelphia: Mason Crest, 2005.

Bellenir, Karen, ed. *Diet Information for Teens: Health Tips About Diet and Nutrition.* Detroit: Omnigraphics, 2001.

Bickerstaff, Linda. *Nutrition Sense: Counting Calories, Figuring Out Fats, and Eating Balanced Meals.* New York: Rosen Publishing, 2005.

Clarke, Julie M., and Ann Kirby-Payne. *Understanding Weight and Depression: A Teen Eating Disorder Prevention Book.* New York: Rosen Publishing, 2000.

Gay, Kathlyn. *Am I Fat?: The Obesity Issue for Teens.* Berkeley Heights, NJ: Enslow, 2006.

Heller, Tania. *Overweight: A Handbook for Teens and Parents.* Jefferson, NC: McFarland, 2005.

Hovius, Christopher. *The Best You Can Be: A Teen's Guide to Fitness and Nutrition.* Philadelphia: Mason Crest, 2005.

Lawton, Sandra Augustyn, ed. *Eating Disorders Information for Teens: Health Tips About Anorexia, Bulimia, Binge Eating, and Other Eating Disorders.* Detroit: Omnigraphics, 2005.

Shanley, Ellen L., and Colleen A. Thompson. *Fueling the Teen Machine.* Palo Alto, CA: Bull Publishing, 2001.

Silate, Jennifer. *Planning and Preparing Healthy Meals and Snacks: A Day-to-Day Guide to a Healthier Diet.* New York: Rosen Publishing, 2005.

Web Sites

The following Web sites are especially good for finding information on nutrition, health, and weight management.

American Diabetes Association

http://www.diabetes.org

Includes information and research on diabetes, a diabetes risk test, tips on exercise and weight loss, nutrition information, recipes, and more.

American Dietetic Association

http://www.eatright.org

Provides education on nutrition and weight control. Click on Find a Nutrition Professional in Your Area.

American Heart Association

http://www.americanheart.org

Gives information about keeping the heart healthy, facts on diseases and conditions, diet and exercise tips, and more. Under the Healthy Lifestyle link, look for the special section for children and youth.

American Obesity Association

http://www.obesity.org

Provides information for the general public and health professionals; advocates for the rights of obese persons. Especially useful are the links Fast Facts and Childhood Obesity.

Food and Nutrition Information Center

http://www.nal.usda.gov/fnic

Resources on food and nutrition for consumers, nutrition and health professionals, and educators. Click on Topics A-Z and then on Adolescence to find links to articles and Web sites especially for young people. Topics there include nutrition, body image, and fitness.

MyPyramid

http://www.mypyramid.gov

The United States Department of Agriculture's Web site on the food guide pyramid includes an explanation of MyPyramid, dietary guidelines, tips for making healthful food choices, and a special section for kids. The site also provides interactive tools with which to design your own healthy eating plan and to track your eating.

National Association of Anorexia Nervosa and Associated Disorders

http://www.anad.org

Information and resources on eating disorders, including binge eating disorder/compulsive overeating, hotline counseling, support groups, referrals to health-care professionals, chat rooms, and more.

National Association to Advance Fat Acceptance

http://www.naafa.org

Advocates on behalf of obese persons to improve quality of life and reduce discrimination. Offers publications and videos on size acceptance, self-esteem, health, and fitness. Click on the Information Brochures link to read about weight loss, diets, eating disorders, and more.

Nemours Foundation: TeensHealth

http://www.kidshealth.org/teen

Teen-oriented information on everything from food and fitness to mental and physical health. In the Search box, type "weight management" to get a list of articles on exercise, losing weight, health issues, obesity, diet plans, body mass index, and more.

Nutrition on the Web (NOW!) for teens

http://www.library.advanced.org/10991/teen9.html

Interactive site created by teens for teens using Mount Sinai Hospital nutrition information and resources. Gives information on exercise, nutrition, teen health, recipes, and more. An interactive section includes a Diet Planner, a Calorie Database, and a Basal (Resting) Metabolic Rate Calculator.

Shape Up America!

http://www.shapeup.org

Promotes awareness of obesity as a health issue. Provides general information and an interactive weight control and physical activity program. Start with the Shape Up! link.

Weight-control Information Network

http://www.win.niddk.nih.gov/

The site says that it provides "up-to-date, science-based information on weight control, obesity, physical activity, and related nutritional issues." Click on Publications: For the Public for an extensive list of pamphlets that can be read online.

BIBLIOGRAPHY

Ahmed, Syed M., Mark E. Clasen, and John F. Donnelly. "Management of Dyslipidemia in Adults." *American Family Physician*, vol. 57, no. 9 (May 1, 1998). http://www.aafp.org/afp/980501ap/ahmed.html (accessed 3-22-07).

American Diabetes Association. http://www.diabetes.org
———. "Type 2 Diabetes in Children and Adolescents." *Diabetes Care*, vol. 23, no. 3 (2000): 381—389.

American Dietetic Association. "Position of the American Dietetic Association: Very-Low-Calorie Weight Loss Diets." *Journal of the American Dietetic Association* 90 (1990): 722-726.

American Heart Association. http://www.americanheart.org
———. "High Blood Pressure, Factors That Contribute To." http://www.americanheart.org/presenter.jhtml?identifier=4650 (accessed 3-22-07).

Barlow, Sarah E., and William H. Dietz. "Obesity Evaluation and Treatment: Expert Committee Recommendations." *Pediatrics*, vol. 102, no. 3 (Sept. 1998). http://www.pediatrics.org/cgi/content/full/102/3/e29 (accessed 3-22-07).

Boutelle, Kerri, et al. "Weight Control Behaviors Among Obese, Overweight, and Nonoverweight Adolescents." *Journal of Pediatric Psychology*, vol. 27, no. 6 (2002): 531—540.

Brownell, Kelly D. "The Environment and Obesity." In Fairburn and Brownell, 433—438.

Centers for Disease Control and Prevention. http://www.cdc.gov

———. "Overweight and Obesity: Obesity Trends: U.S. Obesity Trends 1985–2005." http://www.cdc.gov/nccdphp/dnpa/obesity/trend/maps/index.htm (accessed 3-22-07).

Cronin, Colleen. "Restrictive Operations (Stomach Stapling or Gastric Banding)." http://www.webmd.com/hw/weight_control/hw252781.asp (accessed 3-22-07).

Dietz, William H., and Loraine Stern, eds. *American Academy of Pediatrics Guide to Your Child's Nutrition*. New York: Villard, 1999.

Fairburn, Christopher G., and Kelly D. Brownell, eds. *Eating Disorders and Obesity: A Comprehensive Handbook*, 2nd ed. New York: Guilford Press, 2002.

Favor, Lesli J. *Everything You Need to Know About Growth Spurts and Delayed Growth*. New York: Rosen Publishing, 2002.

Food and Nutrition Board, Institute of Medicine of the National Academies. *Dietary Reference Intakes for Energy, Carbohydrate, Fiber, Fat, Fatty Acids, Cholesterol, Protein, and Amino Acids*. Washington, DC: National Academies Press, 2005.

Gibson, Penny, et al. "An Approach to Weight Management in Children and Adolescents (2–18 Years) in Primary Care." *Journal of Family Health Care*, vol. 12, no. 4 (2002): 108–109.

Grilo, Carlos M. "Binge Eating Disorder." In Fairburn and Brownell, 178—182.

Guyton, Arthur C. *Textbook of Medical Physiology*, 8th ed. Philadelphia: W. B. Saunders, 1991.

Hensrud, Donald D., ed. *Mayo Clinic: Healthy Weight for Everybody*. Rochester, MN: Mayo Clinic Health Information, 2005.

————. *Mayo Clinic on Healthy Weight*. Rochester, MN: Kensington Publishing, 2000.

Hill, James O., and John C. Peters. "Environmental Contributions to the Obesity Epidemic." *Science*, vol. 280 (May 29, 1998): 1371—1374.

Latner, Janet D., and Albert J. Strunkard. "Getting Worse: The Stigmatization of Obese Children." *Obesity Research*, vol. 11, no. 3 (March 2003): 452—456.

Lawson, Willow. "The Obesity-Depression Link." *Psychology Today*. http://www.psychologytoday.com/articles/pto-20030527-000010.html (accessed 3-22-07).

Lowry, Richard, et al. "Weight Management Goals and Use of Exercise for Weight Control among U.S. High School Students, 1991—2001." *Journal of Adolescent Health* 36 (2005): 320—326.

Manson, Joann E., Patrick J. Skerrett, and Walter C. Willett. "Epidemiology of Health Risks Associated with Obesity." In Fairburn and Brownell, 422—428.

Mayo Clinic Staff. "Weight-loss Pills" http://www.mayoclinic.com/health/weight-loss/HQ01160 (accessed 9-22-06).

Mellin, Alison E., et al. "Unhealthy Behaviors and Psychosocial Difficulties Among Overweight Adolescents: The Potential Impact of Familial Factors." *Journal of Adolescent Health*, vol. 31 (2002): 145–153.

National Center for Health Statistics. "Obesity Still a Major Problem, New Data show." http://www.cdc.gov.nchs/pressroom/04facts/obesity.htm (accessed 3-22-07).

National Center for Health Statistics. "Prevalence of Overweight Among Children and Adolescents: United States, 1999–2002." http://www.cdc.gov/nchs/products/pubs/pubd/hestats/overwght99.htm (accessed 3-22-07).

National Center for Health Statistics. "Prevalence of Overweight and Obesity Among Adults: United States, 1999–2002." Figure 2. http://www.cdc.gov/nchs/products/pubs/pubd/hestats/obese/obse99.htm (accessed 3-22-07).

National Digestive Diseases Information Clearinghouse. "Your Digestive System and How It Works." http://www.digestive.niddk.nih.gov/ddiseases/pubs/yrdd (accessed 3-22-07).

National Heart, Lung, and Blood Institute. Obesity Education Initiative. http://www.nhlbi.nih.gov/about/oei/index.htm (accessed 3-22-07).

National Institute of Diabetes and Digestive and Kidney Diseases of the National Institutes of Health. http://www.niddk.nih.gov (accessed 3-22-07).

Needham, Belinda L., and Robert Crosnoe. "Overweight Status and Depressive Symptoms During Adolescence." *Journal of Adolescent Health,* 36 (2005): 48—55.

Paxton, Raheem J., Robert F. Valois, and J. Wanzer Drane. "Correlates of Body Mass Index, Weight Goals, and Weight-Management Practices Among Adolescents." *Journal of School Health*, vol. 74, no. 4 (April 2004): 136—143.

Pi-Sunyer, F. Xavier. "Medical Complications of Obesity in Adults." In Fairburn and Brownell, 467—472.

Rodgers, Ellie. "Gastric Bypass." http://www.webmd.com/hw/weight_control/hw252819.asp (accessed 3-22-07).

———. "Obesity: Surgery." http://www.webmd.com/hw/weight_control/aa51122.asp (accessed 3-22-07).

Seidell, Jacob C., and Marja A. R. Tijhuis. "Obesity and Quality of Life." In Fairburn and Brownell, 388—392.

Shuman, Tracy, editor. "Weight Loss: Is Weight Loss Surgery for You?" http://www.webmd.com/content/Article/46/2731_1656.htm (accessed 9-21-06).

Smolin, Lori A., and Mary B. Grosvenor. *Nutrition and Eating Disorders*. Philadelphia: Chelsea House, 2005.

———. *Nutrition and Weight Management*. Philadelphia: Chelsea House, 2005.

Tamborlane, William V., ed. *The Yale Guide to Children's Nutrition*. New Haven: Yale University Press, 1997.

Texas Department of Health. "Physiological Impact of Obesity on School-Age Children." July 2004. http://www.dshs.state.tx.us/phn/pdf/Physiological%20Conse quences%20of%20Pediatric%20Obesity.pdf (accessed 3-22-07).

United States Department of Agriculture. http://www.mypyramid.gov (accessed 3-22-07).

United States Department of Health and Human Services. "Choosing a Safe and Successful Weight-loss Program." http://www.win.niddk.nih.gov (accessed 3-22-07).

United States Department of Health and Human Services: Overweight and Obesity: "At a glance: The Facts About Overweight and Obesity." http://www.surgeongeneral.gov/topics/obesity/ calltoaction/fact_glance.htm (accessed 3-22-07).

United States Department of Health and Human Services. "The Surgeon General's Call to Action to Prevent and Decrease Overweight and Obesity." htttp://www.surgeongeneral.gov/topics/obesity/ (accessed 3-22-07).

World Health Organization, "Measuring Quality of Life." http://www.who.int/mental_health/media/68.pdf (accessed 3-22-07).

Yanovski, Susan Z. "Binge Eating in Obese Persons." *See* Fairburn and Brownell, 403—407.

INDEX

ABOUT THE AUTHOR

Lesli J. Favor has written eleven books on science, biography, and history topics for young people, including *Food As Foe: Nutrition and Eating Disorders* in this series. She also has published numerous books and workbooks on grammar, writing, and test preparation in English Language Arts. She has a BA in English from the University of Texas at Arlington and an MA and PhD, both in English, from the University of North Texas. She lives in the Seattle area with her husband, son, two dogs, and horse.